THE SOUND OF MORMONISM

THE SOUND OF MORMONISM

A MEDIA HISTORY OF LATTER-DAY SAINTS

Jared Farmer

LEONARD J. ARRINGTON
MORMON HISTORY LECTURE SERIES
NO. 28

Sponsored by

Special Collections & Archives
Merrill-Cazier Library
Utah State University
LOGAN

Copyright 2025
All rights reserved.
ISBN 978-1-64642-703-1 (paperback)
https://doi.org/10.5876/781646427031
Library of Congress Subject Headings: Church of Jesus Christ
of Latter-day Saints—History | Latter-day Saints—History |
Latter-day Saints—Music—History and criticism | Latter-day
Saints—Public opinion | Race—Religious aspects—Church of Jesus
Christ of Latter-day Saints—History | Gender identity—Religious
aspects—Church of Jesus Christ of Latter-day Saints—History
| Mass media—Religious aspects—Church of Jesus Christ of
Latter-day Saints | Radio broadcasting—Religious aspects |
Sound—Religious aspects—Latter-day Saints | Tabernacle (Salt
Lake City, Utah) | Mormon Tabernacle Choir—History.

Published by Merrill-Cazier Library
Distributed by Utah State University Press
Logan, Utah 84322

CONTENTS

PREFACE

This is an annotated and greatly expanded version of a lecture delivered on October 5, 2023, in Logan, Utah, at Utah State University's Russell/ Wanlass Performance Hall. The live version of my Arrington Lecture, billed as "Music & the Unspoken Truth," included more than thirty digital sound files played over the speaker system; the event resembled a podcast, albeit unrecorded. The authorial voice of this mini-monograph, meant to be heard in the mind, is more formal than the "radio voice" performed in Logan, though careful readers will detect echoes of the spoken word.

For inspiration, I name Gladys Clark Farmer Fetzer, my mother, a most faithful organist, and Richard White, my mentor, a most skeptical historian. For the invitation and local arrangements, I thank Jennifer Duncan and Trina Shelton. For help with research, my appreciation to the staff of the Church History Library, including Shawna Fluckiger, Matt Grow, Jeff Thompson, and Rick Turley. For comradeship, my gratitude to Richard Bushman, Hal Cannon, Judith Freeman, Sally Gordon, David Lewis, Ben Park, Greg Smoak, and especially Kim Walters. Amanda Beardsley and Connor Kenaston kindly shared files. Matt Bowman, Michael Hicks, Katie Lofton, Patrick Mason, and John Durham Peters graciously saved me from errors, excluding mine that remain. For prompting me to see the foreign in the familiar, I treasure Magdalena Mączyńska. For line editing, I am thankful again for Amyrose McCue Gill. At Utah State University Press, Laura Furney managed the editorial process. I could not have completed this work without two short-term residencies at two extraordinary places. My respects to Jenny Emery Davidson and Martha Williams for opening the Ernest and Mary Hemingway House to me a second time, and to Louise Excell and Logan Hebner for trusting me to be the inaugural guest at Zion Canyon Mesa.

https://doi.org/10.5876/781646427031.c000

THE SOUND OF MORMONISM

1

THE FIRST AUDITION

In Mormon thought, the Restoration and the Last Dispensation began about two centuries ago, in or around 1820, when a farm boy named Joseph Smith received a celestial transmission after kneeling to pray among sugar maples in western New York. Following the Prophet's martyrdom in 1844, his followers began to call this world-historical moment in a woodlot—the origin, as it were, of modernity—the First Vision.[1]

In media terms, a more appropriate descriptor would be the First Audition.[2] In a draft of his life narrative, Smith recalled bowing down in "the silent grove," then being distracted by "the noise of walking" from an unseen adversary.[3] In the later canonical account, Smith likewise emphasized the auditory as much as the visionary—a triumph of godly speaking over demonic tongue-tying. "I saw two Personages, whose brightness and glory defy all description, standing above me in the air," he wrote. "One of them spake unto me, calling me by name and said, pointing to the other—*This is My Beloved Son. Hear Him!*"[4]

After this and other auditions as prophet, Smith became a medium between Heaven and Earth and employed various media devices—including seer stones—to amplify the communication of the "restored gospel." The Book of Mormon (1830) was a meta-media event: a typeset version of an edited manuscript derived from a handwritten transcription of an oral dictation of a device-assisted translation of hieroglyphic engravings on golden plates that themselves were compilations and abridgements of ancient records, including transcripts of speeches of prophets of old speaking as mouthpieces of God.[5] On April 6, 1830, the day the Church of Christ was organized in Fayette, New York, the translator of the new American scripture received a revelation that began: "Behold, there shall be a record kept among you."[6] Those words now hang in relief above the

https://doi.org/10.5876/781646427031.c001

entrance to the reading room of the Church History Library in Salt Lake City, Utah, a state-of-the-art facility where I did much of my research. The history of this church—renamed by Smith as The Church of Jesus Christ of Latter-day Saints (LDS)—has been, in significant part, a history of broadcasting the Restoration, making records of that work, and archiving those records in multiple redundant formats. For, as the Prophet taught, "Whatsoever you record on earth shall be recorded in heaven, and whatsoever you do not record on earth shall not be recorded in heaven."[7]

It is no exaggeration, then, to proclaim: the prophetic medium is the message of Mormonism; or, more plainly, Mormonism, like all religion, *is* media.[8]

In media studies, scholars use a special adjective to describe the kind of sound that is heard without the cause of the sound being seen: *acousmatic*.[9] Latter-day Saints have a distinctive record of producing as well as receiving such sounds. My research has focused on music and speech performances transmitted by radio waves from the Salt Lake Tabernacle, the temple of LDS broadcasting.[10] Two programs stand out. One is General Conference, the semiannual gathering in April and October when the faithful listen—in person or to a live transmission or to simulcast recordings on delayed broadcast—to solemn addresses by Church leaders, with choral interludes. The other is a weekly offering, *Music and the Spoken Word*—radio's longest-running program, approaching its hundredth anniversary—featuring the Tabernacle Organ and Choir at Temple Square, and an ecumenical message by a commenter.

The entire LDS experience, from the Book of Mormon to *The Book of Mormon* (the satirical Broadway musical from 2011), can be narrated—as attempted here—through sound, which includes music making, voice making, and also muting. In religious importance, these core "sound effects" currently fall in this rank order:

1. *Vocality*, especially the voices of priesthood authority.
2. *Quietude*, especially the stilling of voices that should not be heard.
3. *Music*, especially the "hymns of the Restoration," most especially when performed quietly.

There was a time, though, circa 1932 to 1964, when the combination of semiclassical music and quasi-secular speech, broadcast nationally on the Columbia Broadcasting System (CBS), was the Church's most consequential sound production. In the period defined by the Great Depression, World War II, and the early Cold War, the LDS image turned upside down, from off-white, un-American deviance to pure-white, all-American wholesomeness. *Music and the Spoken Word* altered the sonic, aural, musical, and political trajectory of Mormonism. Today, long after its peak, this radio program continues to affect the outer perception and the inner experience of Latter-day Saints. Well into the internet era, at the dawn of AI-mediated augmented reality, the international membership of the LDS Church inhabits a soundsphere defined by major network AM radio of the 1930s.

In short, Mormons hear God as an old-fashioned radio voice; and, in general, they prefer old media, even when using new media.[11]

According to LDS theology, the divisible—that is, polytheistic—godhead can communicate audibly to Earth; and a living prophet can hear Father or Son and rebroadcast His and/or His miraculous sounds with his own voice, or proxies thereof. This is a theology of "vocal vicariousness."[12] As the Lord spoke through Joseph Smith: "My word shall not pass away, but shall all be fulfilled, whether by mine own voice or by the voice of my servants, it is the same."[13] Thus, Joseph could appoint his counselor Sidney Rigdon to communicate as "spokesman," much like Moses delegated to Aaron.[14] Smith's prophetic dictations were published in newspapers and later canonized in a scriptural book, the Doctrine and Covenants, but the essential orality of his revelations remains. In contrast to the Reformation emphasis on literacy and the Enlightenment privileging of sight, Latter-day Saints, like evangelical Protestants, brought back the premodern sound of God—the spoken word—and rebroadcast it through modern media. The extra-evangelical difference is that Mormonism, a textbook "new religious movement," included a prophet. If Jesus had been the Word incarnate, Joseph Smith was the bodily mouthpiece of the resurrected Jesus.[15]

In the early days of the Restoration, hearing, more than seeing, was believing. Only eleven eyewitnesses were permitted to behold the artifactual Book of Mormon, though the nature of their "vision" with their "eyes" has been a matter of debate ever since.[16] In non-visionary mode, earwitnesses heard the rustle of the shrouded object's metallic leaves.[17] More to the point, LDS peoplehood derived from the public experience of divine orality. In Smith's conception of "theodemocracy," the voice of the people could literally be the voice of God (*vox populi, vox Dei*) so long as the people hearkened to the voice of the prophet-president.[18] When Brigham Young assumed the mantle of emergency leader, edging out Rigdon, he led the majority faction of Latter-day Saints—minus Smith's immediate family—into the "wilderness" of the Great Basin without personal or popular certitude that he had the same mandate as Joseph to speak for God. In time, Utah Mormons in their adopted "promised land" began narrating miracle stories—retrospective, apocryphal, sincere—that buttressed Brother Brigham's credentials as spokesman. Saints who had attended a pivotal meeting in the succession crisis following the lynching of the Prophet now recalled that Brigham, their Moses, had transfigured into the likeness and unmistakable voice of Joseph. A beloved hymn written about the founder, "Come, Listen to a Prophet's Voice, and Hear the Word of God," could now be sung about his successor and the next successor in turn.[19]

In 1897, on the fiftieth anniversary of the exodus, ninety-one-year-old prophet Wilford Woodruff, the fulcrum between Brigham Young's dynastic church and the post-polygyny corporate church, spoke into a "talking machine" so that posterity might know his testimony and the very tone of his voice. Woodruff dictated a statement to an assistant, who punched it out on the Church's typewriter, and then Woodruff read it aloud into the horn of an Edison phonograph. In the online catalog of the Church History Library, the digitized version of the magnetic tape transcription of the phonographic playback of the wax cylinders that contain the grooves etched by the needle propelled by Woodruff's audition bears the ordinal call number "AV 1." Strikingly, this sound file—the original audio recording of an LDS president—includes an account of a speech by the founding seer, Joseph Smith. "I am the only man now living in the flesh who heard that testimony from his mouth," spoke Woodruff, "and I know that it was true by the power of God manifest to him."[20]

Could an elderly Woodruff still hear in his mind the sound of Smith's testimony given more than five decades before? Strangely, few descriptions of Joseph's voice exist. Given his family background, his speech presumably had the accent and tempo of a Vermonter, which was slower than that of a New Yorker. After a mob knocked out one of his front teeth, a soft whistle accompanied his oratory.[21] Lorenzo Snow, fifth president of the LDS Church, recalled that Smith's prophetic voice, diffident at first, became stronger and louder over time.[22] Apostle Parley P. Pratt remembered allegorically that the Prophet, in a moment of righteous anger, "spoke in a voice of thunder, or as the roaring lion."[23] But an outsider described Smith's regular voice as "low and soft."[24]

These contrasts are apropos. In the Abrahamic tradition, God modulates between two registers. One, the still small voice, is ever so soft: a thin silence, a piercing whisper, a murmur, a sigh, a breeze. The other is a great rush, a whirlwind, a thundering, the noise of many waters.[25]

Historically, when revering this God, Catholics made sounds at various levels of intensity, from silent adoration to liturgical plainsong to trumpeted acclamation. Many dissenting Protestants, by contrast, emphasized inaudible worship. In the United States in the nineteenth and early twentieth centuries, evangelical Protestantism and its unacknowledged fraternal twin, Mormonism, followed similar sonic trajectories: from charismatic speaking and singing in tongues to proper playing of organ, choral, and classical music. But when born-agains embraced worshipful clangor in the rock-'n'-roll era, Latter-day Saints stayed the course of aural respectability to the eventual point of sonic peculiarity. As evangelicalism became more roaring in its reverence—and charismatic again—Mormonism became hushed. The emblematic Angel Moroni that stands atop LDS temples blows a trumpet with no sound.

Loudness is not the same as intensity, measured in decibels. The same sound—the cry of a baby, the call of a bird, the feedback from an electric guitar—can be perceived as loud or soft depending on the individual, the group, the cultural context, the spatial setting, the time of day, and so on. Acoustician Harvey Fletcher authored a foundational article in 1933 that defined loudness as a "psychological term" for the "magnitude of an auditory sensation." For purposes of sound engineering, Fletcher tried to express loudness mathematically for the "typical observer" in a "typical condition," but, in real life, loudness was always contingent.[26] In contemporary Mormonism, the inverse of loudness is quietude, which is not the same as silence. Quietude is the dampening of irreverent sounds—that is, noise.

The all-male upper hierarchy of the LDS Church, the First Presidency and the Quorum of the Twelve Apostles, intone softly. These fifteen men—all sustained as "prophets, seers, and revelators" and known colloquially as "the Brethren"—expect their followers to listen quietly, and they encourage LDS mothers and fathers to teach their children didactic songs that equate reverence with stillness. In practice, though, the trinity of vocality, quietude, and music exists in unresolvable tension. At various moments in LDS history, different figures and factions—including musical educators, bureaucrats, and anti-feminists—have emphasized one kind of sound over another and used new media to advance their vocalic and aural agendas. As mediated by today's soft-spoken revelators and echoed by the larger group of male Church functionaries known as General Authorities, the voice of God is barely audible without electric amplification. That may seem ironic, but there is in fact a nineteenth-century theological foundation for the twentieth-century technological turn to quietude. When setting up the School of the Prophets, Smith had received acoustical instructions from the Lord: teachers should be placed so "that the congregation in the house may hear his words carefully and distinctly, not with loud speech."[27]

The founding prophet's attitude toward loudness—and enthusiasm more generally—was ambivalent and site-specific. In the setting of temple worship, he instructed the new covenant people to avoid loud laughter; his book of revelations contains unambiguous passages about the Lord's displeasure with intemperate laughing.[28] Yet, when dedicating a temple—the closest thing to Heaven on Earth and thus most worthy of reverence—Smith gave Latter-day Saints special dispensation to bring sonic intensity: the "Hosanna Shout." Individual ecstatic shouting had been a common feature of the Second Great Awakening, the context for the beginning of Mormonism. As a mature prophet, Smith looked back on his youth, when he had "wanted to get Religion too[,] wanted to feel & shout like the Rest but could feel nothing."[29] Even before founding the Church, he had given a divine commandment to Martin Harris to "preach, exhort, declare the truth, even with a loud voice, with a sound of rejoicing, crying—Hosanna, hosanna, blessed be the name of the Lord God!"[30] This kind of personal and spontaneous outburst became the communal and ritualized Hosanna Shout, first performed in Kirtland, Ohio, at the 1836 dedication of the original temple—a consecrated space where Lorenzo Snow recalled hearing the "singing of heavenly choirs" and the voice of Jesus, "like the sound of many waters."[31] Another earwitness described a "noise" in the temple like "the sound of a rushing mighty wind," which moved people to speak in tongues.[32] At subsequent temple dedications and various other momentous occasions, nineteenth-century Saints let out the sacred shout.[33]

Circumstances prevented early LDS congregants from being un-loud. They lacked acoustical buildings during their journey of tribulations from Ohio to Missouri to Illinois to northern Mexico (future Utah Territory), as they tried to escape the "odium so commonly attached to the sound of mormonism."[34] There was little recourse to ambient silence on the plains and in the mountains: authorities shouted encouragements and admonitions about the Gathering of Zion over buzzing flies and shrieking winds.

Besides, as they waited for the world's end, the Saints rejoiced in song and dance.

NOTES

1 For introductions to LDS history and theology, start with Jan Shipps, *Mormonism: The Story of a New Religious Tradition* (Urbana: University of Illinois Press, 1985); Matthew Bowman, *The Mormon People: The Making of an American Faith* (New York: Random House, 2012); Benjamin E. Park, *American Zion: A New History of Mormonism* (New York: Liveright, 2024).

2 Here I am in accord with Sharon J. Harris and Peter McMurray, "Sounding Mormonism," *Mormon Studies Review* 5 (2018): 33–45.

3 Dean C. Jessee, Mark Ashurst-McGee, and Richard L. Jensen, eds., *The Joseph Smith Papers: Journals*, vol. 1: *1832–1839* (Salt Lake City: The Church Historian's Press, 2008), 87–88; also available at josephsmithpapers.org.

4 Joseph Smith—History 1, 16–17, from the Pearl of Great Price (one of the four "standard works" of LDS scripture), original emphasis. For context, see Dean C. Jessee, "The Early Accounts of Joseph Smith's First Vision," *BYU Studies* 9.3 (Spring 1969): 275–294. For biography, start with Richard L. Bushman, *Joseph Smith: Rough Stone Rolling* (New York: Knopf, 2005). The woodlot has been known as the "Sacred Grove" since the first decade of the twentieth century.

5 See, among other works, Terryl L. Givens, *By the Hand of Mormon: The American Scripture That Launched a New World Religion* (New York: Oxford University Press,

2002); Samuel Morris Brown, *Joseph Smith's Translation: The Words and Worlds of Early Mormonism* (New York: Oxford University Press, 2020); William Davis, *Visions in a Seer Stone: Joseph Smith and the Making of the* Book of Mormon (Chapel Hill: University of North Carolina Press, 2020); Michael Hubbard MacKay, Mark Ashurst-McGee, and Brian Hauglid, eds., *Producing Ancient Scripture: Joseph Smith's Translation Projects in the Development of Mormon Christianity* (Salt Lake City: University of Utah Press, 2020).

6   Doctrine and Covenants (D&C) 21:1.

7   D&C 128:8. See also John Durham Peters, "Recording beyond the Grave: Joseph Smith's Celestial Bookkeeping," *Critical Inquiry* 42.4 (Summer 2016): 842–864.

8   Here I echo Rosemary Avance, "The Medium Is the Institution: Reflections on an Ethnography of Mormonism and Media," from "Forum: Mormonism as Media," *Mormon Studies Review* 5 (2018): 17–72, esp. 60–66. For entry points into Mormon media studies, see Sherry Pack Baker, "Mormon Media History Timeline, 1827–2007," *BYU Studies* 47.4 (2008): 117–123; Peter McMurray, "A Voice Crying from the Dust: The Book of Mormon as Sound," *Dialogue* 48.4 (Winter 2015): 3–44; John Durham Peters, "Mormonism and Media," in *The Oxford Handbook of Mormonism*, ed. Terryl L. Givens and Philip L. Barlow (New York: Oxford University Press, 2015), 407–421; Amanda Beardsley, "Celestial Mechanics: Technologies of Salvation in the Church of Jesus Christ of Latter-day Saints and American Culture" (PhD dissertation, Binghamton University, Binghamton, NY, 2019); Mason Kamana Allred, *Seeing Things: Technologies of Vision and the Making of Mormonism* (Chapel Hill: University of North Carolina Press, 2023); Gavin Feller, *Eternity in the Ether: A Mormon Media History* (Urbana: University of Illinois Press, 2023); Rosemary Avance, *Mediating Mormons: Shifting Religious Identities in the Digital Age* (Salt Lake City: University of Utah Press, 2024). The larger academic "turn" to "media as religion" and the "mediatization of religion" is at least one generation old, as marked by the appearance of the *Journal of Media and Religion* in 2002.

9   See Brian Kane, *Sound Unseen: Acousmatic Sound in Theory and Practice* (Oxford: Oxford University Press, 2014). This Pythagorean term became an academic keyword thanks to musicologist Pierre Schaeffer and film theorist Michel Chion.

10   John Durham Peters, "'My Ancestors Welling in Me': Sound and Silence in the Salt Lake Tabernacle," *Sound Studies* 6.2 (2020): 114–129. For an introduction to sound studies through recording media, see Jonathan Sterne, *The Audible Past: Cultural Origins of Sound Reproduction* (Durham, NC: Duke University Press, 2003).

11   Or, as Gavin Feller put it in a chapter title, "God Is Wireless"; see *Eternity in the Ether*, 55–68. For introductions to voice studies, see Jody Kreiman and Diana Sidtis, eds., *Foundations of Voice Studies: An Interdisciplinary Approach to Voice Production and Perception* (Malden, MA: Wiley-Blackwell, 2011); Nina Sun Eidsheim, *Sensing Sound: Singing and Listening as Vibrational Practice* (Durham, NC: Duke University Press, 2015); Anne Karpf, *The Human Voice: How This Extraordinary Instrument Reveals Essential Clues about Who We Are* (New York: Bloomsbury, 2006); Paddy Scannell, *Why Do People Sing? On Voice* (Cambridge: Polity, 2019).

12   Jake Johnson, *Mormons, Musical Theater, and Belonging in America* (Urbana: University of Illinois Press, 2020), esp. 9–18.

13   D&C 1:38.

14   D&C 100:9.

15   For context, see Leigh Eric Schmidt, *Hearing Things: Religion, Illusion, and the American Enlightenment* (Cambridge, MA: Harvard University Press, 2000). The theology of orality is well beyond the scope of my research, but interested readers can consult Stephen H. Webb, *The Divine Voice: Christian Proclamation and the Theology of Sound* (Grand Rapids, MI: Brazos, 2004) and the oeuvre of Walter J. Ong.

16   Conventionally, they are called the "Three Witnesses" and the "Eight Witnesses," with Mary Whitmer a possible twelfth witness. See Steven C. Harper, "The Eleven Witnesses," in *The Coming Forth of the* Book of Mormon: *A Marvelous Work and a Wonder*, ed. Dennis L. Largey, Andrew H. Hedges, John Hilton III, and Kerry M. Hull (Salt Lake City: Deseret Book, 2015), 117–132.

17   See Richard L. Bushman, *Joseph Smith's Gold Plates: A Cultural History* (New York: Oxford University Press, 2023), 53–54.

18   See Patrick Q. Mason, "God and the People: Theodemocracy in Nineteenth-Century Mormonism," *Journal of Church and State* 53.3 (Summer 2011): 349–375.

19   See Richard S. Van Wagoner, "Making of a Mormon Myth: The 1844 Transfiguration of Brigham Young," *Dialogue* 28.4 (Winter 1995): 1–24. The author of the hymn was Joseph S. Murdock.

20   See Richard Neitzel Holzapfel and Stephen H. Smoot, "Wilford Woodruff's 1897 Testimony," in *Banner of the Gospel: Wilford Woodruff*, ed. Alexander L. Baugh and Susan Easton Black (Salt Lake City: Deseret Book, 2010), 326–363; Philip Lyon Walker, "Dust-Covered Testimonies: The Phonograph and Its Role in the L.D.S. Church Prior to April, 1939" (1968), copy in Church History Library (CHL), Salt Lake City.

21   Lynne Watkins Jorgensen, comp., "The Mantle of the Prophet Joseph Passes to Brother Brigham: A Collective Spiritual Witness," *BYU Studies* 36.4 (1996–1997): 125–204, esp. 167–168.

22   Lorenzo Snow, "Reminiscences of the Prophet Joseph Smith," *Deseret Semi-Weekly News* (Salt Lake City), December 23, 1899, 1.

23   "Joseph Smith a Prisoner," *Latter-day Saints' Millennial Star* 16.33 (August 19, 1854), 525–526.

24   *Daily Evening Gazette* (St. Louis), April 26, 1844, quoted in John Quincy Adams, *The Birth of Mormonism* (Boston: Gorham, 1916), 103.

25   Less frequently in the Torah (and the Book of Mormon), God hisses. For context on the Lord's quiet mode, see Diarmaid MacCulloch, *Silence: A Christian History* (London: Allen Lane, 2013).

26   Harvey Fletcher and W. A. Munson, "Loudness, Its Definition, Measurement, and Calculation," *Journal of the Acoustical Society of America* 5.2 (October 1933): 377–430.

27   D&C 88:129.

28   D&C 59:15, 88:69, 88:121.

29   Alexander Neibaur, Journal, May 24, 1844, CHL, available at josephsmithpapers.org.

30   D&C 19:37. See also D&C 36:3, 39:19.

31   Eliza R. Snow Smith, *Biography and Family Record of Lorenzo Snow* (Salt Lake City: Deseret News Company, 1884), 11. A favorite scripture of Latter-day Saints is Job 38:7, where the Lord speaks of Creation, "when the morning stars sang together, and all the sons of God shouted for joy."

32   Franklin D. Richards, ed., *A Compendium of the Doctrines of the Gospel*, 3rd. ed. (Salt Lake City: George Q. Cannon and Sons, 1898), 268. See also John W. Welch, ed.,

Opening the Heavens: Accounts of Divine Manifestations, 1820–1844 (Salt Lake City: Deseret Book, 2005).

33   See Steven H. Heath, "The Sacred Shout," *Dialogue* 19.3 (Fall 1986): 115–123; Jacob W. Olmstead, "From Pentecost to Administration: A Reappraisal of the History of the Hosanna Shout," *Mormon Historical Studies* 2.2 (Fall 2001): 7–37.

34   "Letter from James Adams, 4 January 1840," *The Joseph Smith Papers: Documents*, vol. 7: *September 1839–January 1841*, ed. Matthew C. Godfrey, Spencer W. McBride, Alex D. Smith, and Christopher James Blyth (Salt Lake City: Church Historian's Press, 2018), 105–07; also available at josephsmithpapers.org.

2

THEY CAME SINGING

"Pioneer children sang as they walked and walked and walked and walked," sing LDS children today. The image is not apocryphal.[1]

The Saints have always been a singing people. When Joseph Smith, in the voice of the Lord, instructed his (first) wife, Emma, to compile a hymnal, he said: "The song of the righteous is a prayer unto me."[2] Music—not painting, not poetry—is mentioned repeatedly in LDS revelation. "And it shall come to pass," spoke the Alpha and Omega through Joseph, His medium, "that the righteous shall be gathered out from among all nations, and shall come to Zion, singing with songs of everlasting joy."[3] The prophet's mother, Lucy Mack Smith, sang in tongues in the ancient language of Moroni, a Book of Mormon prophet, a first-person voice that was translated and later versified into a hymn.[4] This kind of oral performance was hardly unique. According to the recollection of Emmeline B. Wells, the Prophet would listen "spell bound" in his "days of trial and gloom" to the rare voice of young convert Elizabeth Ann Whitney, who had a "prophetic and poetic temperament" and could sing in the "pure Adamic" language—a charismatic gift verified by Smith.[5]

Conventional music more than charisma distinguished Latter-day Saints from contemporary evangelicals. Many revivalists argued against all singing—or against choral singing, solo signing, or instrumental accompaniment. By contrast, Latter-day Saints embraced a variety of musical expressions, especially choral singing, though their choir leaders were essentially conductors, not cantors. Tellingly, at the Kirtland dedication, a choir performed *inside* the temple, the Holy of Holies. A decade later, as the persecuted Saints prepared to abandon Nauvoo, Illinois, their half-built religious capital on the Mississippi River, they made a point of finishing not only the Nauvoo Temple but also the Nauvoo Concert Hall. Dedicated in

March 1845, the hall served as a venue for a short-lived series of extravaganzas with choirs, brass bands, and string ensembles. As Heber C. Kimball proclaimed in an Illinois sermon on music, "God is a God of variety."[6]

Brigham Young's hell-fearing Methodist father had believed in the gift of tongues but did not allow his children to *listen* to a fiddle, much less to dance. It seems remarkable, then, that Young's one and only canonized revelation, "The Word and Will of the Lord"—organizational instructions to the 1847 advance party on their trek to the Great Basin—includes a recommendation to "praise the Lord with singing, with music, with dancing."[7] In vernacular mode, he later put it this way: "Whoever goes to hell I'll warrant you won't here [*sic*] fiddling or have dancing . . . all music is in heaven, all enjoyment is of the Lord."[8]

When lawyer Thomas L. Kane made an inspection of the Saints at their winter squatters' camp on Omaha tribal land, he already knew about the "peculiar fondness of the Mormons for music," yet still he was astonished to hear "Mendelssohn Bartholdy, away there in the Indian Marches!"[9] These westering Saints also sang a rousing hymn of their own: "The Upper California, O that's the land for me / It lies between the mountains and great Pacific Sea." The lyrics went on to imagine the sound of hosannas ringing in the western hills and valleys and "our cousin Lemuel" joining the Saints "hand & hand" to usher in the millennium.[10]

After their arrival in unceded Shoshone and Ute homelands—giving a sacred shout as they entered the Valley of the Great Salt Lake—members of the Camp of Israel became sound bringers and silencers, too. They brought the noise of industry: the chopping of trees, the bleating of sheep, the mooing of cows, the snorting of oxen, the splitting of solid quartz monzonite, the hammering of pegs and nails, the gurgle of irrigation ditches, the discharge of guns. Systematically, they worked to eradicate animal predators that howled and yipped and roared and called.[11]

For a short but significant period, Latter-day Saints attempted to ally with the "Lamanites" or "cousin Lemuel," as they called Native peoples in the theological abstract, using Book of Mormon categories. The names derived from Laman and Lemuel, ancient progenitors of Amerindians—who, like Latter-day Saints, were chosen people of Israelite lineage, albeit a fallen branch that needed to be restored.[12] When Utah's

Indigenous inhabitants refused to play the role of Lamanites, LDS settlers proved adept at recategorizing them as "hostile Indians" and killing them. In 1850, immediately after the first such exterminatory campaign, Young and his advisers convened in the tipi of Sowiette, an important Nuche (Ute) leader, near the mouth of the Provo River in Utah Valley. The Saints performed two hymns, ending with their foremost anthem of pioneering, "All Is Well" (now known as "Come, Come, Ye Saints"). Overcome with the "Great Spirit," Young spoke in tongues. When he asked his hosts if they understood the spiritual language, they all said yes. That evening, Utes returned the favor, singing and dancing in a circle.[13] When reporting on this encounter back in Great Salt Lake City, Brother Brigham expressed characteristic ambivalence. Utah Valley had the "meanest & lowest class of Indians," yet it was the Saints' obligation to teach them, feed them, and "do good unto them." A choir then sang the "Indian hymn."[14]

Over the next two decades, the LDS practice of Zionism—gathering the new covenant people to the new chosen land—prevailed over the theology of Lamanites as Hebraic descendants, the very "seed of Israel." As tens of thousands of British and Danish converts arrived, creating pressure for land, Young went back on LDS prophecies and promises concerning the "redemption" of the "red brethren": he worked with the US government to remove from Utah Territory's main settlement corridor Utes and other Numic peoples who spoke and chanted and sang and drummed in non-Western tones and rhythms.[15] The prophet also began admonishing his followers against excess glossolalia, including xenoglossia of purported Lamanite languages.

In the Articles of Faith (1842), written for an outside audience, Smith had stated, "We believe in the gift of tongues." However, for his home audience, he sometimes had to rein in the exuberance with qualifications such as "do not indulge too much" and "be not so curious about tongues."[16] This LDS charismatic practice originated in Ohio and became a serious reputational problem in the Missouri phase of the Church, even before the scandalous introduction of plural marriage.[17] Both heterodoxies survived Joseph Smith. One recollected account of summer 1847 depicts Eliza R. Snow pacing a cabin floor to control her heavy breathing during a meeting in which a male associate prophesied in an "Indian tongue" regarding the imminent destruction of the wicked United States.[18] Once she had composed herself, Snow responded in the "pure language" of Eden, with translation by Zina D. H. Young.[19] Sister Snow and Sister Young—close friends who each were sealed in marriage to *both* Joseph Smith and Brigham Young—often auditioned like this, in addition to performing woman-to-woman healing rituals.[20]

Such reports disturbed and confused outsiders, much like polygyny did. How could Anglos who erected concert halls, opera houses, theaters, and organs—seemingly civilized white people who championed life-long education and universal suffrage—how could they possibly behave in such outlandish, heathenish ways? The US Protestant establishment, including all three branches of government, applied enough coercive power—imprisoning Church leaders, seizing Church assets—that Woodruff capitulated on plural marriage in 1890, issuing "the Manifesto" against new polygamous sealings.[21] The practice of glossolalia required nothing so formal. By the 1893 dedication of the Salt Lake Temple—a sonic showcase, including a new "Hosanna Anthem" to complement the Hosanna Shout—this gift of the spirit was gradually quieting down on its own.[22] Speaking and singing in tongues had never been central to the religion like "celestial marriage," and surely the practice embarrassed some of the cultured British converts who did so much to build up the musical infrastructure of Utah Territory.

The three successive music directors of the Salt Lake Tabernacle—an edifice open to the public, unlike the adjacent temple—were British-born musicians with professional training: George Careless, Ebenezer Beesley, and Evan Stephens. All three were hymn composers, too, and they—along with Charles John Thomas, Thomas C. Griggs, Joseph J. Daynes, and John E. Tullidge—formed a British American musical hierarchy in Salt Lake City that helped define what Latter-day Saints called "mountain home" music.[23] As of the 1870 census, a quarter of Utah Territory's population comprised immigrants from the British Isles. This population structure helps explain why the chroniclers of pioneer Utah hailed the first locally produced opera, *H.M.S. Pinafore* in 1879, as a momentous artistic event, second only to the coming of *Messiah* in 1875.[24]

The British American standard-bearers did much to codify the sound of LDS hymnody. The two oldest hymnals—one published in the US, the other in the UK, the latter going through many editions—had contained lyrics only: poetic lines with standard meters that could be set to any number of tunes, though mostly English Protestant tunes, to be sung in unison. In their first fifty years of congregational singing, US-born Latter-day Saints put less energy into composing music than penning original lyrics to express their unusual doctrines. Some of these "songs of Zion" began as translations of singing in tongues.[25] Starting in the 1880s, LDS composers contributed musical settings to psalmodies, the most popular one published by the Deseret Sunday School Union. Evan Stephens would later describe "Mormonistic" music as an outgrowth of the hymns of English Congregational minister Isaac Watts—the opposite of what the director called the gloomy and lachrymose solemnity of Catholic music.[26]

Many hymn settings by home composers featured four-part vocals. Some congregations could handle these arrangements; others could not. Proximity to Great Salt Lake City was not a perfect predictor. Brigham Young, as part of his colonization scheme, had distributed musical talent throughout the Intermountain West; many remote villages such as Parowan had notable ward (parish) choirs. Music culture became a point of defensive pride among Saints within the "Mormon Corridor." As an LDS magazine editorialized on "musical progress" in 1896: "If the civilization of a people is indicated by its advancement in the arts and sciences, Utah is by no means behind the rest of the country."[27]

By the radio era, most Latter-day Saints could sing in parts; that was a musical legacy of British converts, particularly Welsh ones like Stephens. He taught British choral society techniques—and spread the ambition to sing Handel and Haydn—to children in Logan and Salt Lake City before he assumed directorship of the flagship choir; even then, he continued to work with children's choirs through the Sunday School. Stephens knew how make sweet music with non-professionals. The Salt Lake Tabernacle Choir had been, in its original form, a church choir, because the Tabernacle in its opening decades was used for standard sacrament services on Sundays. The choir did not regularly give concerts and did not go on tour until Stephens took charge in 1890. He added hundreds of members to the rolls of the choir and regularly performed with 300+ singers, billed as THE LARGEST CHURCH CHOIR IN THE WORLD.[28] The majority of the members were women, because Stephens made it a five-part group, with first and second sopranos. Many of his singers—including Lizzie Thomas Edward, who often sang solos—were Wales-born, too. It is not much of an overstatement to say that Welsh immigrants took the Nauvoo singing tradition and magnified, institutionalized, and Mormonized it.[29]

Stephens's tenure coincided with a great transformation of the LDS Church, for the "whiskerless and wifeless Mormon" took the Tabernacle baton in the immediate aftermath of the Manifesto.[30] Utah finally achieved statehood a few years later. Between 1890 and 1930, the reputations of Mormonism and the Beehive State fluctuated as different constituencies acted at cross-purposes. From the inside, many Latter-day Saints wanted to proactively Americanize their religion on progressive LDS terms; reactionary elements wished to maintain the old-time religion on the down-low until Jesus returned, and some of the latter hived off into fundamentalist groups. From the outside, women's rights advocates and evangelicals (overlapping categories) continued to denounce the faith, while pragmatic Republicans and profit-minded industrial capitalists created alliances with LDS powerbrokers.[31]

To the extent that Latter-day Saints succeeded in rehabilitating their image before the Great Depression (when the Church's internal Welfare Plan received good press), they did so through music, especially singing. The rise of choral groups coincided with the decline of martial brass bands, a major feature of Mormon culture from the 1830s through the 1890s. A dress rehearsal for the new sound occurred in 1891 at a "Grand Concert" in Salt Lake City, when the Tabernacle Choir performed a march and chorus from Bellini's *Norma* as well as a settler-colonial glee song by Stephens called "Vales of Deseret" (using the original proposed name for the Territory and State of Utah):

> Once these vales were but a dreary waste.
> Sweet, tuneful lays these hills had never heard.
> The sound of howling wolves, dread beasts of prey,

Chimed with the Indian's savage cry of war,
While nature wept to be by art adorned . . .
                    Tra la la etc.[32]

In 1893, Woodruff sent a large contingent of the great choir to the World's Columbian Exposition in Chicago, the first major eastward land trip by Latter-day Saints since Brigham Young and his followers deserted Illinois in 1847, when Chicago barely existed. The prophet called the choir members on a mission; he expected of them the highest comportment. The choir's desired effect was visual as well as aural. The sight of 250 well-scrubbed young ladies and gentlemen in color-coordinated formal wear—a look that communicated cleanliness and healthiness—served to defy outsider allegations of bodily and racial degeneracy caused by polygyny. To the anti-Mormon claim that Saints had horns, the Church countered eugenically with its "intelligent and superior-looking" choir.[33] One Illinois journalist admitted his "overwhelming curiosity to know what manner of creature a real live flesh and blood Mormon is" and prepared his readers for disappointment, for "these musical Mormons are just the same as other people."[34]

In Chicago, the choir competed in the "International Eisteddfod," a competitive music festival organized by Welsh American chapters of the Honourable Society of Cymmrodorion. In the mixed choir division, the pool with most prize money, the Saints won silver. This was a stupendous outcome, notwithstanding the fact that only four choirs participated, two of them from the great center of Welsh American culture—Scranton, Pennsylvania. Following this relative triumph, the Tabernacle Choir accepted an invitation to sing at the dedicatory placement of the Liberty Bell, on loan to the White City from the City of Brotherly Love. Before the iconic cracked bell, Stephens led the mega-choir in a rendition of "The Star-Spangled Banner."[35]

Warm publicity about music contrasted with the Church's cold reception at another event held in conjunction with the Columbian Exposition: the World's Parliament of Religions. Whereas the Church's singing missionaries won a prize at the International Eisteddfod, the official delegation could not even get in the door of the parliament, an international assembly with a mission to promote interfaith dialogue. The conveners did not consider Mormonism a religion, much less a world religion. Speaking Saints, unlike singing Saints, remained pariahs.

The LDS Church worked with what it had. Following the Chicago experience, the First Presidency (the president-prophet plus two senior apostolic counselors) wrote a memo that defined the choir's purpose—an ecclesiastical PR proclamation that still stands. Choir members were missionaries, explicitly; their music service took precedence over all other duties; and those called to sing should faithfully and cheerfully attend practice with discipline to maintain the ensemble's strong reputation with the goal of becoming the highest exponent of the "Divine Art" in all the land. Through artistic perfection, the choir would unstop the ears of thousands now deaf to the truth, thus removing prejudice and dispelling ignorance. In the face of misrepresentation, the choir had to be ready at all times to reflect the excellence, beauty, intelligence, order, and refinement of the people of God.[36]

In line with this mission statement, the Salt Lake Tabernacle hosted a national eisteddfod in 1895. One of Brigham Young's granddaughters, Emma Lucy Gates, won a prize in the competition and went on to study in Europe, becoming a noted opera singer.[37] Another eisteddfod took place in Utah in 1898. In between these Welsh American music festivals, in 1896, the First Presidency sent the choir to the Bay Area for eight concerts, its first tour. Once again, the prophet personally set the singers apart as missionaries. With expositions multiplying across the land, the Mormon "monster chorus" made a habit of attending them.[38] It traveled to Seattle in 1909 for the Alaska-Yukon-Pacific Exposition and back to Chicago in 1911 for a National Irrigation Congress, where the choir performed organist John J. McClellan's thirty-minute "National Ode to Irrigation," preceded by "Worthy Is the Lamb" from *Messiah* and an arrangement of "Dixie."[39]

Stephens and his volunteer singers developed a type of programming and performing that would persist through the decades, even as the repertoire expanded. The non-professional choir sang a little bit of this, a little bit of that, all performed in uniform style—an aesthetic of cheerful moderation—making everything sound vaguely the same. Perfection in the divine art would remain forever out of reach when, in Marxian terms, musical missionaries provided unpaid overtime labor to the corporation of the Church: working with amateurs, Stephens could not hope to develop a repertoire of full-length choral works beyond *Messiah* (Handel), *The Creation* (Haydn), and *Elijah* (Mendelssohn). In 1896, he toured the Bay Area with a classical pops variety show: duets, trios, quartets, organ pieces, violin solos, Scottish airs and ballads, scenes from Donizetti, Verdi, and Meyerbeer, and—above all—choral anthems by Evan Stephens himself. Near the end of his career, the music director wrote unequivocally that programs of the "light type" would not be tolerated by his home audience, for the tastes of Latter-day Saints had risen above the level of the "frivolous" and "trashy" music heard in other cities.[40] (That included Utah cities, where in-migration and immigration due to the mining sector had temporarily diluted the dominance of Latter-day Saints.) Stephens's code language signified that he hated Tin Pan Alley—even though he loved light opera. This was a fine distinction to uphold, but he tried, and so would his successors. They participated in a larger, longer quest to change the image of Mormonism from ignominy to respectability. Even as the lines between "classical" and "popular" became defined in the late nineteenth century and then became blurred in the late twentieth century, the premier LDS choir carried on with a conservative middle approach.[41]

The first phonographic recordings of the Tabernacle Organ and Choir, made in 1910, showcase an already established Mormon middlebrow eclecticism. The choir sang original LDS hymns, the "Hallelujah Chorus," and Victor Herbert's "Gypsy Love Song." This was perhaps the only time the organist played fortissimo in an accompanying role, for that was the only way to get enough sound into the horn of the recording machine. In solo mode, McClellan played the first three minutes of Bach's Toccata and Fugue in D minor, BWV 565, as well as a ditty called "Gondoliers," from *A Day in Venice*, Opus 25, by the very minor American composer Ethelbert Nevin.[42]

God remained a God of variety—in moderation, that is.

NOTES

1 Elizabeth Fetzer Bates, "Pioneer Children Sang as They Walked" (1957), in *Children's Songbook* (Salt Lake City: The Church of Jesus Christ of Latter-day Saints, 1989), 214.

2 Doctrine and Covenants (D&C) 25:12.

3   D&C 45:71.

4   The hymn was called "Moroni's Lamentation." See Michael D. Hicks, "Music and Heaven in Mormon Thought," in *The Oxford Handbook of Mormonism*, ed. Terryl L. Givens and Philip D. Barlow (New York: Oxford University Press, 2015), 498–512.

5   Emmeline B. Wells, "Elizabeth Ann Whitney," *Woman's Exponent* 10.20 (March 15, 1882): 1–2. For context, see Jennifer Reeder, "The Textual Culture of the Nauvoo Female Relief Society Leadership and Minute Book," in *Foundational Texts of Mormonism: Examining Major Early Sources*, ed. Mark Ashurst-McGee, Robin Jensen, and Sharalyn D. Howcroft (New York: Oxford University Press, 2018), 154–189.

6   Quoted in Darrell Babidge, "The Nauvoo Music and Concert Hall: A Prelude to the Exodus," *BYU Studies* 58.3 (2019): 58–77, quote on 68.

7   D&C 136:28.

8   Young on January 16, 1848, quoted in John G. Turner, *Brigham Young: Pioneer Prophet* (Cambridge, MA: Harvard University Press, 2012), 164.

9   Thomas L. Kane, *The Mormons* (Philadelphia: King & Baird, 1850), 32–33. In this context, "Marches" means borderlands.

10   John Taylor wrote the words, which appeared in various hymnals. For context and a facsimile of the lyrics, see Matthew J. Grow, Ronald K. Esplin, Mark Ashurst-McGee, and Jeffrey D. Mahas, eds., *The Joseph Smith Papers, Administrative Records: Council of Fifty, Minutes, March 1844–January 1846* (Salt Lake City: The Church Historian's Press, 2016), 401–404.

11   For context, see Benjamin Lindquist, "Testimony of the Senses: Latter-day Saints and the Civilized Soundscape," *Western Historical Quarterly* 46.1 (Spring 2015): 53–74; John T. Coleman, *Vicious: Wolves and Men in America* (New Haven, CT: Yale University Press, 2008), 173–87.

12   See Jared Farmer, "Displaced from Zion: Mormons and Indians in the Nineteenth Century," *Historically Speaking* 10.1 (January 2009): 40–42; Amanda Hendrix-Komoto, *Imperial Zions: Religion, Race, and Family in the American West and the Pacific* (Lincoln: University of Nebraska Press, 2022). Latter-day Saints were hardly the only ones with such ideas; see Elizabeth Fenton, *Old Canaan in a New World: Native Americans and the Lost Tribes of Israel* (New York: New York University Press, 2020); Matthew W. Dougherty, *Lost Tribes Found: Israelite Indians and Religious Nationalism in Early America* (Norman: University of Oklahoma Press, 2021).

13   Jared Farmer, *On Zion's Mount: Mormons, Indians, and the American Landscape* (Cambridge, MA: Harvard University Press, 2008), 78–80.

14   "Historian's Office general Church minutes, 1839–1877," May 26, 1850, CR 100-318, box 2, fd. 20, Church History Library (CHL), Salt Lake City, available at https://catalog .churchofjesuschrist.org.

15   See, among other works, Sondra G. Jones, *Being and Becoming Ute: The Story of an American Indian People* (Salt Lake City: University of Utah, 2019); Will Bagley, ed., *The Whites Want Every Thing: Indian-Mormon Relations, 1847–1877* (Norman, OK: Arthur H. Clark Company, 2019).

16   "Discourse, 28 April 1842," in *The First Fifty Years of Relief Society: Key Documents in Latter-day Saint Women's History*, ed. Jill Mulvay Derr, Carol Cornwall Madsen, Kate Holbrook, and Matthew J. Grow (Salt Lake City: The Church Historian's Press, 2016),

208; "Gift of the Holy Ghost," *Times and Seasons* (Nauvoo, IL), June 15, 1842, 823–826, quote on 825; both sources also available at josephsmithpapers.org.

17   See Lee Copeland, "Speaking in Tongues in the Restoration Churches," *Dialogue* 24.1 (Spring 1991): 13–33; Dan Vogel and Scott C. Dunn, "'The Tongue of Angels': Glossolalia among Mormonism's Founders," *Journal of Mormon History* 19.2 (Fall 1993): 1–34; Mark Lyman Staker, *Hearken, O Ye People: The Historical Setting for Joseph Smith's Ohio Revelations* (Salt Lake City: Greg Kofford Books, 2009); J. Spencer Fluhman, *A Peculiar People: Anti-Mormonism and the Making of Religion in Nineteenth-Century America* (Chapel Hill: University of North Carolina Press, 2012), esp. 55–58; Terryl L. Givens, *Feeding the Flock, the Foundations of Mormon Practice: Sacraments, Authority, Gifts, Worship* (New York: Oxford University Press, 2017), 213–256.

18   For context, see Christopher James Blythe, *Terrible Revolution: Latter-day Saints and the American Apocalypse* (New York: Oxford University Press, 2020).

19   Presendia Lathrop Kimball, "A Venerable Woman," *Woman's Exponent*, June 1, 1883, 2. See also Maureen Ursenbach Beecher, ed., *The Personal Writings of Eliza Roxcy Snow* (Logan: Utah State University Press, 2000), 176; Matthew W. Dougherty, "None Can Deliver: Imagining Lamanites and Feeling Mormon, 1837–1847," *Journal of Mormon History* 43.3 (July 2017): 22–45.

20   For context, see Linda King Newell, "Gifts of the Spirit: Women's Share," in *Sisters in Spirit: Mormon Women in Historical and Cultural Perspective*, ed. Maureen Ursenbach Beecher and Lavina Fielding Anderson (Urbana: University of Illinois Press, 1987), 111–150; Martha Sonntag Bradley and Mary Brown Firmage Woodward, *4 Zinas: A Story of Mothers and Daughters on the Mormon Frontier* (Salt Lake City: Signature Books, 2000); Jonathan A. Stapley and Kristine Wright, "Female Ritual Healing in Mormonism," *Journal of Mormon History* 37.1 (Winter 2011): 1–85; Laurel Thatcher Ulrich, *A House Full of Females: Plural Marriage and Women's Rights in Early Mormonism, 1835–1870* (New York: Knopf, 2017); Derr et al., *The First Fifty Years of Relief Society*; Jonathan A. Stapley, *The Power of Godliness: Mormon Liturgy and Cosmology* (New York: Oxford University Press, 2018), 79–104.

21   D&C Official Declaration 1. Non-compliance with the Manifesto necessitated a "Second Manifesto," issued at General Conference in April 1904. For context, see B. Carmon Hardy, *Solemn Covenant: The Mormon Polygamous Passage* (Urbana: University of Illinois Press, 1992); Sarah Barringer Gordon, *The Mormon Question: Polygamy and Constitutional Conflict in Nineteenth-Century America* (Chapel Hill: University of North Carolina Press, 2002); Christine Talbot, *A Foreign Kingdom: Mormons and Polygamy in American Political Culture, 1852–1890* (Urbana: University of Illinois Press, 2013); Kathryn Gin Lum, *Heathen: Religion and Race in American History* (Cambridge, MA: Harvard University Press, 2022).

22   See James X. Allen, "Passing of the Gift of Tongues," *Improvement Era* 8.2 (December 1904): 109–111.

23   G. Careless, E. Beesley, J. J. Daynes, E. Stephens, and T. C. Griggs, comps., *The Latter-day Saints' Psalmody: A Collection of Original Tunes* (Salt Lake City: Deseret News, 1896), preface.

24   For overviews of LDS music history, see Lowell M. Durham, "The Role and History of Music in the Mormon Church" (MA thesis, University of Iowa, Iowa City, 1942),

copy in CHL; Lowell M. Durham, "On Mormon Music and Musicians," *Dialogue* 3.2 (1968): 19–40; Michael Hicks, *Mormonism and Music: A History* (Urbana: University of Illinois Press, 1989); Terryl L. Givens, *People of Paradox: A History of Mormon Culture* (New York: Oxford University Press, 2007), 117–142, 253–263; Michael Hicks, *Spencer Kimball's Record Collection: Essays on Mormon Music* (Salt Lake City: Signature Books, 2020).

25 See Frederick G. Williams, "Singing the Word of God: Five Hymns by President Frederick G. Williams," *BYU Studies* 48.1 (2009): 57–88.

26 Evan Stephens, "Songs and Music of the Latter-day Saints," *Improvement Era* 17 (June 1914): 760–767.

27 "Musical Progress in Utah," *Millennial Star* 58.39 (September 24, 1896): 617–618, quote on 618.

28 *Grand Concert by the Tabernacle Choir in the Large Tabernacle, Friday, Feb, 27. '91* (Salt Lake City, 1891), copy in Special Collections, Firestone Library, Princeton University, Princeton, NJ; also available on Google Books.

29 "Welsh Origins of the Mormon Tabernacle Choir," CR 252-11, fd. 2, CHL.

30 Undated quote from "Mormon Tabernacle Choir publicity file, 1911–1967," CR 352-19, CHL. On Stephens's sexuality, see D. Michael Quinn, *Same-Sex Dynamics among Nineteenth-Century Americans: A Mormon Example* (Urbana: University of Illinois Press, 2001).

31 On this period, see Thomas G. Alexander, *Mormonism in Transition: A History of the Latter-day Saints, 1890–1930* (Urbana: University of Illinois Press, 1986); Armand L. Mauss, *The Angel and the Beehive: The Mormon Struggle with Assimilation* (Urbana: University of Illinois Press, 1994); Kathleen Flake, *The Politics of American Religious Identity: The Seating of Senator Reed Smoot, Mormon Apostle* (Chapel Hill: University of North Carolina Press, 2004).

32 *Grand Concert by the Tabernacle Choir in the Large Tabernacle.*

33 George Q. Cannon, "The Tabernacle Choir at the World's Fair," *Juvenile Instructor* 28.18 (September 15, 1893): 566–569, quote on 567.

34 *Chicago Sunday Tribune*, September 4, 1893, quoted in E. H. Peirce, comp., *Mormon Tabernacle Choir, Being a Collection of Newspaper Criticisms and Cullings* (Salt Lake City: self-published, 1910), 6–7, copy in Firestone Library. For context, see W. Paul Reeve, *Religion of a Different Color: Race and the Mormon Struggle for Whiteness* (New York: Oxford University Press, 2015).

35 See Reid Neilson, *Exhibiting Mormonism: The Latter-day Saints and the 1893 Chicago World's Fair* (New York: Oxford University Press, 2011).

36 Paraphrased from First Presidency to Members of the Tabernacle Choir, February 11, 1895, in James R. Clark, comp., *Messages of the First Presidency*, vol. 3 (Salt Lake City: Bookcraft, 1966), 267–268.

37 In sources, she is often listed as Lucy Bowen, after the family name of her eventual husband, Albert E. Bowen, an apostle in the LDS Church. See Catherine M. Johnson, "Emma Lucy Gates Bowen: Singer, Musician, Teacher," *Utah Historical Quarterly* 64.4 (Fall 1996): 344–355.

38 "Six Thousand Miles with the 'Mormon' Tabernacle Choir," part 2, *Juvenile Instructor* 47.4 (April 1912): 196–202, quote on 201.

39 "Mormon Chorus Sings Praises of Irrigation," *Chicago Daily Tribune*, October 27, 1911.

40   Stephens, "Songs and Music of the Latter-day Saints."
41   For context, see Keir Keightley, "Music for Middlebrows: Defining the Easy Listening Era, 1946–1966," *American Music* 26.3 (Fall 2008): 309–335.
42   Richard E. Turley Jr., "'Epoch in Musical History': The Mormon Tabernacle Choir's First Recordings," *Utah Historical Quarterly* 79.2 (Spring 2011): 100–121.

3

TABERNACLE AND ORGAN

Told conventionally, the history of music in the Salt Lake Tabernacle becomes a chronicle of the choir: its touring, its radio broadcast, its discography, and its outsized role as a PR-cum-proselytizing arm of the Church. But telling the narrative chorally elides an important period—from the completion of the transcontinental railroad (1869) through the radio debut of *Music and the Spoken Word* (1929). In this sixty-year period, not the choir but the organ was the most famous musical feature of both Mormonism and Utah. The story of the organ is also the story of its unique architectural and acoustical container—the Tabernacle—and the building's impact on how Mormons speak as well as sing.

After laying out the grid for Great Salt Lake City, Latter-day Saints made plans for a temple, a tabernacle, and a theater. The three buildings were completed in reverse order. Because a place for general assembly—a "tabernacle" in LDS usage of the biblical word—had been immediately necessary, settlers erected a wood "bowery" in Salt Lake in July 1847. This open-air shade pavilion remained in use for years. Later came an adobe tabernacle, a squat barn-like building finished in 1852, complete with a small pipe organ—the first such instrument in LDS history. This provisional building became known as the "Old Tabernacle" when its instantly famous successor opened in 1867. As authorized by Brigham Young, the "New Tabernacle" or "Great Tabernacle" featured an unusual design: a self-supporting oval dome without view-blocking pillars. The ellipsoidal room with vaulted ceiling—framed with rawhide-wrapped timbers—was gloomily dark and drearily plain, except for a grand organ (designed by Joseph Ridges, with casework by Ralph Ramsey) at the back, centered behind the pulpit. The building's exterior, by contrast, looked striking, though outsiders often mocked its resemblance to a melon, an

https://doi.org/10.5876/781646427031.c003

egg, an umbrella, a dish cover, a cauldron, a bathtub, a capsized boat, a beached whale, a tortoise. Yet non-Mormons could not stay away from the "Church of the Holy Turtle." Their curiosity was too great.[1]

Visitation to Great Salt Lake City spiked after the joining of the Union Pacific and the Central Pacific at Promontory Summit, Utah, in 1869 and the construction of a spur line to the territorial capital the following year. Gawkers came to Salt Lake on their transcontinental stopover: they voyeuristically tried to spot polygamous families, they admired the Wasatch Range, and they departed with few positive observations about the social landscape. Railroad tourists applauded the industry represented by Mormon irrigation ditches; they took pleasure in the municipal hot springs (and later the lakeside Saltair Resort); and, above all, they loved the acoustic "pin-drop test" in the Tabernacle, followed by an organ recital. This tourist tradition began with concerts for dignitaries and large groups, scheduled in advance. Later, the practice continued on demand; then, in 1901, semi-weekly; then, in 1908, daily at noon (excluding Sundays) from April to October; and finally, in 1916, every non-Sabbath day, with additional evening recitals in the summer.[2]

The current formula for recitals on Temple Square (formerly Temple Block) is very similar to that devised by organist John J. McClellan in the first decade of the 1900s. In turn, McClellan's programming resembled the kind of daily matinee played by leading organists at the 7,000-seat Festival Hall at the World's Columbian Exposition in August–October 1893, a "watershed moment in U.S. organ culture."[3] (McClellan had served as an organ's assistant at the Chicago console and followed that instrument to its final home at the University of Michigan, where he completed his music degree.) The Tabernacle organist now, like then, chooses two or three classical pieces that show off different registers of the instrument, performs an arrangement of an old melody, and does their own take on "Come, Come, Ye Saints." Today's organist plays less from the French romantic repertoire and far fewer (if any) opera transcriptions. Wagnermania has waned. But these are minor differences.[4]

The Tabernacle Organ took its current iconic shape, including more than 10,000 pipes, with a major expansion completed in 1916, during a US fad for "monster organs" bookended by the Wanamaker Organ (1904, moved to a Philadelphia department store after debuting at the St. Louis world's fair) and the Boardwalk Hall Auditorium Organ in Atlantic City, New Jersey (1932, billed as the world's largest and loudest musical instrument). Unlike those two, the Tabernacle Organ grew over time, through multiple renovations. Originally pumped by hand, the wind-powered instrument gained a hydraulic motor in 1875 and an electric one in 1901. The original casing was taller than it was wide. To match the increased width of the 1916 casing, Church architects expanded the choir loft, meaning 337 seats needed to be filled. The choir's standard performing size increased to that exact number, driven by architectural, visual, and social demands rather than musical considerations. Stephens sometimes toured with 400 singers. No choir needs to be that big; indeed, there is a principle of diminishing returns with greater choral size. Synchronization becomes more difficult, and articulation (attack and decay) gets muddier. But a crowd of singers paired well visually with a wall of pipes. The combination looked impressive on postcards (and later on television). Like the body culture on display at the Deseret Gymnasium, or the Church-owned Saltair, or the Church-sponsored annual hike of Mount Timpanogos, the bulked-up organ with massed choir was a sign of Mormon mainstreaming within US culture at a time when bigness meant progress.[5]

In the 1910s and 1920s, every LDS ward with the means raised money to install pipe organs in their chapels, thus contributing to the heyday of organ culture in the United States. Across the Gilded Age and Progressive Era, US Protestants abandoned architectural Calvinism in favor of neo-Gothic luxe; many high-toned places of metropolitan worship featured grand organs behind the pulpit stage, making church more like theater. Then, in the 1920s, movie palaces added Wurlitzer organs, making cinema more like church. Radio City Music Hall in New York City had the largest Wurlitzer, with second place going to the Denver Municipal Auditorium—a secular analog, on the other side of the Rockies, to the Salt Lake Tabernacle. Finally, in the 1940s, Hammond organs began to appear in baseball parks, the arenas of the leading US "civil religion" at the time.[6]

All of this helps explain why, in the early decades of radios and automobiles, the Tabernacle Organ at Temple Square was one of the most famous instruments in the United States as well as a top Utah tourist attraction before the Beehive State had national parks. Latter-day Saints were the first Americans to offer daily organ recitals for free—and now they are among the last to keep up the practice. In the absence of church bells, liturgical organ strains, or calls to prayers, Salt Lake City features a half-hour of keyboard favorites on a five-console, 207-rank instrument at noon.

There are thick layers of folklore, laid down by generations of LDS apologists, about the "perfect acoustics" of the Salt Lake Tabernacle. That would indeed be miraculous if true. Prior to the construction of Boston's Symphony Hall (1900), designed in consultation with physicist Walter Sabine, US architects simply emulated European halls famed for their acoustics.[7] But the Tabernacle was sui generis and was built before Sabine established architectural acoustics as a field of applied physics. The auditorium certainly had better acoustics than would be expected from a concave space with a hard ceiling. Luckily, LDS builders followed standard US building practices, mixing cattle hair into the plaster, which had a sound-absorbing effect. Without this bovine element, the building might have been a disaster. The first technical analysis of the ellipsoidal auditorium, conducted in 1930, resulted in a mixed scorecard, notwithstanding the "very extended reputation of being one of the most acoustically perfect buildings in the world."[8] The building featured both dead spots and whispering galleries. Harvey Fletcher of Bell Labs, a devout Latter-day Saint as well as the most eminent US acoustician after Sabine, could only muster the word *peculiar* to describe the acoustics when quizzed by a General Authority.[9] The nineteenth-century anti-Mormon travel writer T. B. H. Stenhouse got closer to the truth when he described the Tabernacle as "free from every taint of the science of acoustics."[10]

His snark should be qualified. Before amplification in 1923 and especially before the addition of the gallery in 1875, the domed room featured:

- Perfect acoustics for exactly one thing: the famous demonstration of the sound of a pin dropping (onto a table or into a hat), with tourists listening in silence from a position opposite the pin dropper, ~200 feet away.
- Lovely acoustics for solo organ.

+ Challenging acoustics for a choir.
+ Extra-challenging acoustics for choir with organ.
+ Devilish acoustics for its primary purpose: listening to the voices of the prophets.

The same reverberations that made the pin-drop test successful made singing difficult. For example, choir members heard the vibrations from the organ pipes, located above them, at a slight delay—deflected from the opposite wall. Because of the decay of sound over space and time, the accompaniment arrived back to the choir a microtone flat. Therefore, if the choir sang on pitch with respect to the organ they heard, it seemed off pitch with respect to the organ the audience heard. Tabernacle music directors tried acoustical fixes: a string quartet could be placed below the choir, or a small pump organ could be placed among the singers.

The problem of unintelligible speech was harder to fix. At General Conference, the smooth, hard, curved ceiling amplified the shifting of bodies, the shuffling of feet, the chattering of mouths, the crying of babies. After listening at various locations in the new building, architect Truman Angell lamented in his diary, "The busle and noice distroide the words of the speaker or drounded them." After worrying on it, he held out hope that "if the people would be verry still all mite hear."[11] Otherwise pro-natal Brethren tried at first to blame and shame the mothers in the congregation. In 1868, George Q. Cannon, in his role as editor of the *Deseret News*, categorized the bringing of babes in arms to the Tabernacle as a "bad habit" and a "'crying' evil."[12] In 1870, Brigham Young admonished mothers for the "considerable annoyance" of their young children, who belonged at home.[13] A decade and a half later, President John Taylor demanded from the pulpit: "If any of the babies cannot be kept quiet, they must be carried out."[14] His audience cooperated, sometimes; an outsider marveled at the "absolute dumbness" of one congregation, which allowed the "feeble voice" of the Prophet to travel to every ear.[15]

It was easier to change the building than to change people. To dampen the bustle, the Tabernacle's managers tried hanging curtains, flags, buntings, garlands, artificial flowers, leafy festoons, and more. These muffling devices served to enliven the austere interior, but they also collected dust.

The addition of a gallery in 1875 improved the acoustics more than anything had before but simultaneously expanded the capacity—the Church
packed in 10,000 people prior to fire codes—which increased the incidental noise. "It is the wonderful acoustic properties of this house," said senior
apostle Joseph F. Smith in 1899, "that actually makes it so difficult to make
the people hear when there are so many together as are here today, because
every little sound tends to confuse the voice of the speaker."[16]

Everyone agreed that softly spoken words were easier to decipher in the
Tabernacle than loud words, at least under ideal conditions. The building
seemingly impelled Latter-day Saints to carry out their theological imperative to be un-loud. Ironically, small, secular audiences of non-LDS tourists experienced far superior acoustics (the pin-drop test plus recital) than
the multitudes of believers who gathered each April and October. At conferences, General Authorities had little choice but to raise their voices over
all the incidental noise. These pioneer men were practiced in yelling from
years of outdoor oratory. Under the dome, however, greater volume did
not produce greater intelligibility.

The acoustical imperfections of the "Holy Turtle" remained trouble-
some for speakers and listeners in General Conference until 1923, when
the building acquired microphones and loudspeakers. One might have
expected an instant change in vocality, the long-deferred attainment of
"not with loud speech." After outdoor prophets crying in the wilderness,
after semi-outdoor prophets shouting in the bowery and indoor prophets
speaking hoarsely in a noisy auditorium with makeshift drapery, the time
had come for speaking softly with amplification.

It didn't happen instantly. The apostles needed an electrical School of
the Prophets. They needed radio.

NOTES

1   On the history of the building and its use, see Levi Edgar Young, *The Great Mormon
Tabernacle with Its World-Famed Organ and Choir* (Salt Lake City: Bureau of
Information, 1917); Stewart L. Grow, *A Tabernacle in the Desert* (Salt Lake City:
Deseret Book, 1958); Carl W. Condit, "The Mormon Tabernacle," *Progressive Architect*
47 (November 1966): 158–161; Robert C. Mitchell, "Desert Tortoise: The Mormon
Tabernacle on Temple Square," *Utah Historical Quarterly* 35.4 (Fall 1967): 279–291; Paul
H. Peterson, "Accommodating the Saints at General Conference," *BYU Studies* 41.2

(2002): 4–39; Ronald W. Walker, "The Salt Lake Tabernacle in the Nineteenth Century: A Glimpse of Early Mormonism," *Journal of Mormon History* 31.2 (Fall 2005): 198–240; Nathan D. Grow, "One Masterpiece, Four Masters: Reconsidering the Authorship of the Salt Lake Tabernacle," *Journal of Mormon History* 31.3 (Fall 2005): 170–197; Elwin C. Robison with W. Randall Dixon, *Gathering as One: The History of the Mormon Tabernacle in Salt Lake City* (Provo: Brigham Young University Press, 2014); Stewart L. Grow and Scott C. Esplin, *The Tabernacle, "An Old and Wonderful Friend"* (Provo: BYU Religious Studies Center, 2007); David Walker, *Railroading Religion: Mormons, Tourists, and the Corporate Spirit of the West* (Chapel Hill: University of North Carolina Press, 2017), esp. 147–157; Peters, "Sound and Silence in the Salt Lake Tabernacle."

2   See Thomas K. Hafen, "City of Saints, City of Sinners: The Development of Salt Lake City as a Tourist Attraction 1869–1900," *Western Historical Quarterly* 28.3 (Autumn 1997): 342–377. Latter-day Saints also used the Tabernacle for exhibit-style displays of progress and for staged debates between Mormon apologists and anti-Mormons.

3   Anne Laver, "Blending the Popular and the Profound: Organ Concerts at the 1893 World's Columbian Exposition," *Journal of the Society for American Music* 16.2 (May 2022): 153–183, quote on 153. See also Annie Rosella Compton, "John J. McClellan, Tabernacle Organist" (MA thesis, Brigham Young University, Provo, UT, 1951).

4   See Valerie Harris, "How the West Was Won: The Impact of Railroad Tourism on the Development of Pipe Organ Recitals at the Salt Lake Tabernacle" (MA thesis, Arizona State University, Tempe, 2022); Barbara Owen, *The Mormon Tabernacle Organ: An American Classic* (Salt Lake City: The Church of Jesus Christ of Latter-day Saints, 1990); Barbara Owen, "The Maturation of the Secular Organ Recital in America's Gilded Age," *Nineteenth-Century Music Review* 12.1 (June 2015): 95–117.

5   See Timothy Hecker, "The Era of Megaphonics: On the Productivity of Loud Sound, 1880–1930" (PhD dissertation, McGill University, Montreal, Canada, 2014), 45–102; Michael Tavel Clarke, *These Days of Large Things: The Culture of Size in America, 1865–1930* (Ann Arbor: University of Michigan Press, 2007). On Mormon recreational culture in this period, see Farmer, *On Zion's Mount*; Richard Ian Kimball, *Sports in Zion: Mormon Recreation, 1890–1940* (Urbana: University of Illinois Press, 2003); for context, Clifford Putney, *Muscular Christianity: Manhood and Sports in Protestant America, 1880–1920* (Cambridge, MA: Harvard University Press, 2001). Although I'm likening the choir to a body, I should specify that the individual bodies of singers were (and are) thoroughly clothed, practically tented.

6   See Orpha Ochse, *The History of the Organ in the United States* (Bloomington: Indiana University Press, 1975); Craig R. Whitney, *All the Stops: The Glorious Pipe Organ and Its American Masters* (New York: Public Affairs, 2003); Anne C. Loveland and Otis B. Wheeler, *From Meetinghouse to Megachurch: A Material and Cultural History* (Columbia: University of Missouri Press, 2003); Jeanne Halgren Kilde, *When Church Became Theatre: The Transformation of Evangelical Architecture and Worship in Nineteenth-Century America* (New York: Oxford University Press, 2005).

7   See Emily Thompson, *The Soundscape of Modernity: Architectural Acoustics and the Culture of Listening in America, 1900–1933* (Cambridge, MA: MIT Press, 2002).

8   Wayne B. Hales, "Acoustics of the Salt Lake Tabernacle," *Journal of the Acoustical Society of America* 1.2A (January 1930): 280–292, quote on 280.

9   Harvey Fletcher to Marvin O. Ashton, August 18, 1939, Harvey Fletcher Papers, MSS 1233, box 1, fd. 2, Special Collections, Lee Library, Brigham Young University, Provo, UT. At this time, the Church was considering lining the Tabernacle's ceiling with Celotex.

10   T. B. H. Stenhouse, *The Rocky Mountain Saints: A Full and Complete History of the Mormons* (London: Ward, Lock, and Tyler, 1873), 694.

11   "Truman O. Angell journals and record book, 1851–1881," MS 626, Church History Library, Salt Lake City, entry on October 6, 1867.

12   "Bad Habits," *Deseret Evening News* (Salt Lake City), November 17, 1868.

13   Brigham Young, "Proper Conduct in Meeting" (May 5, 1870), *Journal of Discourses* 13 (Liverpool: Horace S. Eldredge, 1871), 343–345.

14   Taylor quoted in Henry W. Lucy, *East by West: A Journey in the Recess*, vol. 1 (London: Richard Bentley and Son, 1885), 106.

15   Joseph Bennett, "Observations on Music in America," *Musical Times* (April 1, 1885): 193–196, quote on 196.

16   Joseph F. Smith, untitled speech, April 9, 1899, in *Sixty-Ninth Annual Conference* (Salt Lake City: Deseret News, 1899), 67.

4

RADIO RELIGION

Latter-day Saints had been anticipating megaphonic if not telephonic communication for decades, given Joseph Smith's revelation that "the sound must go forth from this place into all the world, and unto the uttermost parts of the earth."[1] Although spiritualism did not penetrate Mormon Utah as thoroughly as other milieux, Latter-day Saints responded to the language of the "spiritual telegraph." For example, in 1873, apostle Orson Pratt mused about "something connected" to the mouths and mouthpieces of the seven archangels who would, in the last days, sound their trumpets and speak with "a loud voice": "I do not know that the sound will be so much louder than some we have heard, but it will be carried by some miraculous power so that all people will hear it."[2]

Nathaniel Baldwin, an LDS inventor from Fillmore, Utah, attended General Conference in Salt Lake in 1905 and found it disturbing that he could not make out the words of the Brethren. "I was working on a steam engine device at that time," he later recalled, "and until that day nothing was farther from my mind than the problem of amplifying sound."[3] The Tabernacle's acoustical limitations inspired him to invent the world's first headphone, which led to Utah's first high-tech industry. Baldwin made a fortune on military contracts and consumer products before squandering his wealth on spiritual causes. He rejected the Manifesto. His Omega Investment Company subsidized the emergent polygamous fundamentalist movement and bankrolled a "dream mine" (prospecting for precious ore based on visions related to apocryphal LDS prophecies).[4]

In the post-Manifesto period, more respectable scientific figures rose through the ranks of the LDS hierarchy, and they tried to integrate Marconi's wireless telegraphy into Church teachings. First among them was Norwegian-born, German-trained biochemist and university president

https://doi.org/10.5876/781646427031.c004

John A. Widtsoe, a de facto theologian at a time when LDS theology was in flux. Widtsoe became an apostle after he published his books *Joseph Smith as Scientist* (1908) and *Rational Theology* (1915). Fellow apostle and doctrinal author James E. Talmage was a geologist, dream mine debunker, and another former university president. In the Progressive Mormon moment of the 1920s, Widtsoe and many other college-educated General Authorities spoke semi-scientifically (or semi-spiritualistically) about the importance of being "in tune" or, better yet, "in strict tune," requiring twice-daily kneeling prayer to enable two-way radio communication with God. This was a redefinition of Christian language that went back centuries in English; prior to Marconi, being "in tune with God" (or "tuned to the spirit," and so on) was a musical figure of speech. After Marconi, God's perfectly tuned instrument became the radio. According to Progressive Saints, Joseph Smith had been in perfect tune, hearing a signal with no static. But every person was a potential radio station capable of receiving the Holy Spirit and also transmitting vibrations of the embodied soul over the ether—radio waves that could continue forever into space, speaking to eternity.[5]

Heber J. Grant, who became president of the LDS Church in 1919, was a businessman and radio enthusiast. In 1922, he became the first LDS prophet to speak over the air waves. Broadcasting from the roof of the six-story Union Pacific Building (home of the *Deseret News*), beside the tin shack that served as the headquarters of the scrappy start-up station KZN ("ZN" for Zion), Grant did not introduce himself or provide any introduction for his "message to the people of the world." He just launched into a reading of excerpts from the Doctrine and Covenants. "This is the gospel, the glad tidings which the voice out of the heavens bore record unto us," transmitted the living prophet, in the revealed words of a dead prophet. Lacking any sense of radio theater, Grant ended his radio address abruptly: "This is the end of the quotation. I bear witness to all mankind that Joseph Smith was a prophet of the true and living God." The microphone then went to Grant's wife, who provided, to a historian's ear, the best quote from the broadcast. "I would not be surprised," said Augusta Grant, "if we were talking to the planets before many years."[6]

During Grant's long presidency, Church administration developed a coherent strategy regarding electronic media: to adopt them, to own outlets for them, to produce content for them, and to use them to broadcast General Conference for an internal audience and the Tabernacle Organ and Choir for an external listenership.[7] In 1925, the LDS Church bought a majority stake in KFPT (the former KZN), which soon became KSL ("SL" for Salt Lake).

To succeed in mass communication, the Church needed partners in the business world. The success of KSL during the 1920s and 1930s resulted from the entrepreneurship of General Manager Earl J. Glade. In 1931, he secured from the Federal Radio Commission the strongest permitted signal, 50,000 watts, allowing the AM waves to reach the entire Intermountain West during the day and much farther at night. Glade dreamed of KSL becoming "America's Station." He successfully negotiated with NBC, then CBS, to be an affiliate. (Salt Lake City's strategic location between the Pacific Coast and the Great Plains made its transmission towers vital for coast-to-coast broadcasting.) Locally, Glade started his own production company through which he hired KSL radio players to perform scripted shows and advertisements. What geographers call the "Mormon Culture Region" was reified in the fourth dimension by KSL.[8]

The Church's centennial celebration in 1930 provided a test of this religious radio regionalism. The First Presidency issued directions so that a uniform program could be executed everywhere, simultaneously. At 10:00 a.m. on April 6, the Tabernacle Choir and congregation began by singing "We Thank Thee, O God, for a Prophet"; then President Grant spoke. Within the Tabernacle, hard-of-hearing Saints listened to the Prophet with earphones—a version of Nathaniel Baldwin's invention—that had recently been installed on the back pews under the balcony.[9] To close the event, everyone under the dome arose and performed the Hosanna Shout while waving white handkerchiefs. Congregants inside the Assembly Hall, a different building on Temple Square, did the same—listening to a public address system, as did the overflow audience standing outside by the Seagull Monument. Hundreds of miles away—from eastern Idaho to Southern California—thousands more Latter-day Saints sang and shouted in time in ward chapels equipped with radios. Wards without radio equipment received instructions to read and perform the same centennial program synchronously, as if their bodies were receivers. "Undoubtedly the greatest miracle of the century," said President Grant's script, "is the accomplishment by which the human voice, with the personality of the speaker, may be indefinitely preserved and reproduced."[10]

With a boost from national networks, the Mormon Culture Region expanded invisibly once a week, overlaying the entire country, transmuting into ecumenical form. When *Tabernacle Organ and Choir* began airing on the NBC network in 1929, it was a public-service music program, with the organ getting top billing and most of the airtime. NBC's economic purpose was to create consumer demand for the radios manufactured by its corporate backers GE, Westinghouse, and RCA. Who wouldn't want to hear a mammoth organ in their kitchen or living room? Initially, the novelty factor overrode the sound quality. The Tabernacle owned a single microphone, extended to maximum height atop the pulpit, a placement that forced KSL announcer Ted Kimball to stand on a ladder for the duration of the first broadcast—sent to New York over telephone lines, then retransmitted by radio. The program began and ended with Wagner.

In 1930, when Kimball left on a mission, Glade hired a recently returned missionary—Richard L. Evans, age twenty-four—and instructed him on radio diction. The KSL chief always insisted on "proper language."[11] Initially, Evans's speaking role resembled that of Temple Square recital organists, who introduced their selections. But when the radio program (under a new name, *Thoughtful Sabbath Hour*) moved to CBS in 1932, Evans began experimenting with signature phrases spoken over the choir humming the theme song, "Gently Raise the Sacred Strain." The voice began: "Again, from the Crossroads of the West"; or "From out of the West"; or "We welcome you unto the hills"; or "We beckon your thoughts unto the hills." (*Unto the Hills* was the title of Evans's 1940 anthology with Harper and Brothers, the first of his many books that converted the spoken word to the written word.) The *Salt Lake Tribune* described the format as not a concert presentation but rather a "mildly philosophic unit."[12] Evans invited listeners to receive a "fabric of quiet reflection" from a "place of quiet repose." In time, the Sunday program became known by a phrase Evans used in his intros and outros: *Music and the Spoken Word*.[13]

Much like the later difference between "digitally native" Millennials and "analog" Boomers, Evans, an electrical native, belonged to a different generation than the acoustical elders who ran the Church. Evans quickly learned to speak in the newly standardized radio dialect termed "General American English." He did not, like Heber J. Grant, drawl out Salt Lake City as *Sol Lake Ciddy* and California as *Californy*. And Evans never raised his voice. Early AM radio technology could not handle sonic dynamism, great volume, high notes, and plosive consonants. The medium selected for conversational rather than oratorical speech. KSL technicians labored to get the Brethren to speak "properly," to stay on script, and to end on time. Instead of sitting or standing still and speaking gently into the mike as if addressing an intimate friend, authorities like B. H. Roberts could not stop themselves from pacing about, gesticulating, exhorting, and pounding the table—which only generated dead air, feedback, or blasted circuitry.[14]

Analogously, the muscular voices of opera singers and vaudeville belters fared poorly on early radio. In the late 1920s, stations turned instead to untrained singers—crooners—whose soft, breathy voices paired better with the microphones of the day. The fandom that formed around crooners, the original teen idols, prompted a conservative backlash in the 1930s.[15] The LDS Church participated in this moral panic: a Tabernacle organist, speaking for the Church Music Committee, wrote a piece for the youth magazine denouncing this "reprehensible prostitution of art."[16] Crooners were perceived to be effeminate if not queer, and the fact that their audible sighs and sensual whispers could invade the bedrooms of young people seemed like the antithesis of the still small voice. Eventually, Bing Crosby emerged as a morally acceptable vocal product—a straight masculinist version of a crooner, singing in a lower register. Although Evans conveyed more bookishness than brawniness and never sang, he was in effect the LDS Bing Crosby. Evans, like the crooners, loved the microphone—indeed, he put his face right into it, forming over time a lip groove in the foil—but he sounded like an old man in a suit, not a young dandy. Conservatives across the country welcomed his disembodied baritone into their homes.[17]

The trimly mustachioed Evans was not the only crooner-not-crooning Latter-day Saint broadcasting to metropolitan America. Starting in 1930, missionaries in the Eastern States Mission, headquartered in New York City, began producing fifteen-minute public-service programs for dozens of radio stations in large and small markets throughout the Mid-Atlantic. Years before the Church had a centralized publicity committee, the Eastern States Mission organized its own publicity office and set missionaries apart as publicity officers. Radio stations, which needed to fill airtime, generally accepted offers of free programming.[18] The mission president sought out the advice of Roscoe Grover, former chief announcer at KSL, who had relocated to Brooklyn. Grover penned a series of memos on how to write and produce a program, including "Mechanics of Good Radio Copy" and "Words Which Many of Us Mispronounce" (e.g., *ah-poss-tull* for "apostle" and *ee-piss-tull* for "epistle").[19]

Grover's suggested radio plan for "Mormon Melody and Meditation" was a local version of the national *Music and the Spoken Word*: a theme song, a scripture reading, a hymn, a timely thought to contemplate, another hymn, an announcement. Sometimes missionaries sang the hymns live, following Grover's advice to avoid loudness, crescendos, and "dangerous" high notes. More often, they played DJ, using sixteen-inch discs with selections by the Tabernacle Choir from its CBS program, transcribed "off the line" (from the radio signal) by RCA Victor through a financial arrangement with the Church. As for the readings, Grover recommended a background of soft music, like humming or a harp. "The intimacy of a personal appeal is very effective," he instructed. Avoid "preachiness," which people "tune out." Grover appreciated the auditory efficacy of sister missionaries. He imagined a listener's reaction: "What a sincere and beautiful voice. I wonder what she looks like. You know I'd really like to meet her."[20] This was a benign feminine version of radio's home invasion.

Around 1940, the LDS Church started an internal distribution system of portable record players and sets of its own transcription discs of the choir, recorded directly in the Tabernacle. Missionary-produced radio shows spread to other missions—and other countries—and continued through the 1950s. The person in charge of disc distribution and a million other things was Gordon B. Hinckley, executive secretary of the Radio, Publicity, and Mission Literature Committee, formed in 1935. At that time, he was one of the Church's very few male staffers—the vanguard of a priesthood bureaucracy. Apostles gave him a nickname: "the Slave."[21]

Hinckley did his best to improve the radio quality of General Conference, which had been broadcast by KSL since 1924. Speakers habitually went over time; some of them continued to shout into the mike; and most of them spoke in Utah vernacular. Hinckley's office could mandate practice in vocal modulation by inviting General Authorities to appear on KSL's Sunday evening "Church hour." Higher-profile auditions came on *Church of the Air*, a CBS public-service program that allowed clergymen of "major faiths" to address a national audience in common worship. Numerically, Mormonism did not count as major. By way of comparison, the LDS Church claimed 862,664 members in 1940, while the Catholic Church claimed 21.4 million adherents across the United States, a ratio of 1:25. But in light of the success of *Music and the Spoken Word*, CBS rewarded the LDS Church with four annual slots of free airtime, which was PR manna for a regionalistic minor faith recovering from a century of bad press—not to mention villainous depictions in popular fiction, melodrama, and silent cinema.[22] Hinckley helped select the speakers and worked with the national network to schedule two of the four slots in conjunction with the semiannual conference, in part because the choir could then provide preludes and postludes. The familiar voice of Richard Evans welcomed the radio audience over the humming of the choir. In other words, the Church approached its *Church of the Air* segments as an extension of *Music and the Spoken Word*.[23]

The Federal Radio Commission and the National Association of Broadcasters deserve some credit for the standardization of LDS vocality. According to rules codified in the 1930s, national networks were variety networks that had to provide a certain amount of public-service programming. Some of that free airtime ("sustaining time") had to go to religious organizations, but none of it could be sectarian or controversial. From CBS's position, a Latter-day Saint message on *Church of the Air* should ideally sound, in content and delivery, similar to a Catholic or Methodist message. Born-again Christians could not and would not play by the polite rules of sustaining time, so they formed their own commercial radio stations that could offer God hour every hour. Radio evangelists did not modulate their folksy voices on air or diminish the intensity of their praise. They cared more about bearing witness than pleasing the sound engineer.

Some sectarian radio stars built regional and national audiences—notably Aimee Semple McPherson (aka Sister Aimee) in Los Angeles and Charles Edward Coughlin (aka Father Coughlin, aka the Radio Priest) in Detroit. Initially a smooth-voiced speaker, Coughlin later brought evangelical-like fervor to his populist and apologist Catholic messaging. Tens of millions tuned in to his weekly show in the mid-1930s, when the host harangued the microphone as well as Franklin Delano Roosevelt and Jews.[24]

In Salt Lake City, younger General Authorities successfully worked on their radio voices in the KSL sound booth, but many older ones struggled. This can be heard in the earliest extant electrical transcription of General Conference, recorded off the line from *Church of the Air* in 1936. A CBS radio professional decorously introduces President Grant who, in comparison, sounds *un*professional: he coughs; he preaches like an outdoor preacher; and he uses most of his airtime reciting the transcribed words of Joseph Smith speaking in the voice of the Lord.[25] Perhaps unique among his generational cohort, Grant—born in 1856—did attain a radio voice, though it was not a voluntary result of practice, such as his famous successes turning messy handwriting into gorgeous calligraphy and tone deafness into melodious singing. Even the super-ultra-industrious Grant could not adapt his rapid-fire exhortative speech for the radio—that is, not until he literally lost his voice when he almost died from a series of strokes that left him half paralyzed. When Grant finally returned to public speaking in 1941, people described the transformation as a vocal impairment when, from a radio attitude, it was an improvement. "I shall not speak loud," said Grant, coming through clearly. "By not speaking loud I do not believe it will hurt me."[26]

The first prophet, seer, and revelator to speak softly into the microphone using General American English from the moment he became president of the Church was the media-savvy, PR-conscious, clean-shaven David O. McKay. He was seventy-seven years old at the time of his sustaining in 1951. During the early days of radio, as an apostle, McKay had experienced mike fright: he could not speak naturally on air, even though he could do so over the telephone. "He never sounded like himself in his speeches," remembered Roscoe Grover. "He was shouting and emphasizing and so on."[27] But two decades of listening to Richard Evans had an effect. Although he sometimes slipped back into oratorical style, McKay deliberately softened his voice even as senescence slowed his voice until his timbre finally sounded, in his seventies and eighties, more like the twenty-something Evans of the 1930s.

Back then, Evans had compensated for his youth by over-enunciating, going for gravitas yet still talking at a clip. First Presidency member J. Reuben Clark, a dominant figure who had a decent radio voice, listened to KSL on Sundays and gave Evans critiques. In 1934, Clark complained to his diary that "Richard was too precipitate, not deliberate enough."[28] Decades later, Roscoe Grover would remember the mature Evans as a "good grammarian" with a "sanctimonious" delivery. His voice "was so pious that it had no lift."[29] A longtime member of the choir was a bit more generous in his recollection: Evans's spoken word sounded "soupy" at first but became more "impelling" over time.[30]

Even as broadcast technology improved, allowing for greater dynamic range, Evans barely altered the levelness of his intonation. He had found his radio voice as a young man and he stuck with it, having won popular and professional acclaim (including a Peabody Award in 1943), becoming the most famous voice in the Church—indeed, the most famous *person* in the Church—as well as the best-selling author of ten consecutive quote books with a major New York press.[31] Stacks of fawning fan letters—an industry-approved metric for audience size and engagement—arrived each day, many with the address line "Crossroads of the West." Harry Truman was an admirer. Why would Evans modulate his tone and pitch, even as AM gave way to FM gave way to TV? To prepare each inspirational message, Evans talked into a Dictaphone for ten minutes, then edited down the performance from a transcript of his own recording.[32] By the 1960s, the sound of his "Spoken Word" had become anachronistic, or out of time—though that very constancy was part of the appeal for conservative listeners living through destabilizing times. His obituary in *Time* magazine in 1971 noted that his "low-key sermonettes" stuck to ethics rather than doctrine, so that "many of the show's faithful listeners did not realize that Evans was a Mormon; they considered themselves followers of 'Richard Evans' church.'"[33]

It's instructive to compare Evans to non-LDS near-contemporaries on the radio. Fulton Sheen, the Catholic priest who reached an audience of millions on NBC's *The Catholic Hour* (1930–1952), generally used a tempo that was measured, like Evans, but he was much more homiletic, with a theatrical streak. Paul Harvey, whose daily comments became a fixture on ABC after 1952, was endowed with the "voice of God" or the "sound of amber waves of grain," according to his admirers. He, like Evans, sounded white, straight, conservative, patriarchal. But Harvey added an evangelical timbral style. He was performative and melodramatic, even campy, with a folksy touch. He spoke slowly, then quickly, pausing occasionally for effect; Evans, in contrast, paused consistently as an affect. The KSL cadence, unlike the evangelical one, was decorous, placid, even imperturbable. If Evans sounded avuncular and gentle, Harvey sounded masculine and brawny. No one could mistake the smooth, unaccented voice of Richard L. Evans with the raspy imperatives of clergyman Norman Vincent Peale (of "positive thinking" fame) or the fervid southernisms of celebrity evangelist Billy Graham. In no way did mid-century Latter-day Saints want to be confused with evangelicals—their historic antagonists—or with charismatics. The feeling was mutual. In the same era when preachers like Graham used amplification to exert vocally to throngs of born-again revivalists in outdoor sports arenas and when Jehovah's Witnesses blasted the word of God from loudspeakers on automobiles, General Authorities progressively quieted their Tabernacle voices, projecting electronically to an invisible multitude through radio and television.[34]

Once an amplified President McKay could command reverent silence without loud speech, priesthood leaders below him fell in line with their vocality. After decades of inconsistency, the speaking style of General Conference became standardized. All the way down to the ward level, Latter-day Saints imitated the amplified voice of the prophet. Even children, on rotation, did a ward version of music and the spoken word: they stood in front of the congregation at the microphone and read the monthly "Sacrament Gem," preceded and followed by a four-bar organ prelude and postlude (as published in the Church youth magazine).

Richard L. Evans rarely appears in academic works of LDS history and Mormon studies, but he should. He pioneered the professional sound of prophecy in the age of mechanical reproduction. He provided the voice-work for televised specials about Mormons (e.g., *They Came Singing*) and the proselytizing film *Man's Search for Happiness* shown in the Mormon Pavilion at the 1964 world's fair in New York City. Through the power of his anodyne voice, he was elevated from his radio job to the Quorum of the Seventy (1938) and then to the Quorum the Twelve Apostles (1953), becoming one of the youngest men ever in both bodies, surrounded by men of the acoustical generation. Fittingly, Evans's high leadership slot had opened with the death of J. Golden Kimball, aka the "Swearing Apostle," a leader famous for his irreverent, off-the-cuff speaking; his vernacular style; his cowboy accent; and his reedy upper register that required no microphone to be heard.[35] If Kimball was the voice of nineteenth-century Mormon regionalism, Evans was the voice of twentieth-century LDS organizationalism. As he rose in the hierarchy, his speech changed in one notable way: the words per minute decreased, as if he were imitating McKay's geriatric tempo, even as McKay was emulating Evans's radio cadence. In tandem, these two men created the vocalic template for modern Mormonism.

As an electrical native who landed a job at KSL in the late 1920s, Evans was, from a certain point of view, simply the right man in the right place at the right time. The unspoken truth is this: he was not the most qualified person to give vocal recitations in the Tabernacle. The University of Utah had a Department of Elocution headed by its founder, Maud May Babcock, the first woman on campus hired at the rank of professor. A nationally recognized leader in speech, drama, and physical education, Babcock was also active in the theatrical endeavors of LDS youth. What if this New York–born, single, divorced convert to the Church—a woman who had parrots and Chow Chows instead of children, a professor known for having the most proper speaking voice in the Beehive State—had been chosen to be the choir's commentator? Could she have modulated for the microphone, despite the industry paradigm of a "radio voice" being male? This is not completely idle speculation, for Babcock had accompanied the choir on its first California tour—not to sing but to perform elocution between choral numbers. She recited poems over violin obligato. Arguably, then, Maud May Babcock was the original "Spoken Word." But she performed before the radio age, and no wax cylinder recordings of her readings from 1896 exist.[36]

NOTES

1   Doctrine and Covenants (D&C) 58:64.

2   "Discourse by Elder Orson Pratt," December 28, 1873, *Journal of Discourses* 16 (Liverpool: Joseph F. Smith, 1874), 326–338, quote on 328. See Revelation 14:2–9.

3   "How a Church Service and War Promoted Utah's Radio Industry," *Deseret News*, December 21, 1929.

4   See Merrill Singer, "Nathaniel Baldwin, Utah Inventor and Patron of the Fundamentalist Movement," *Utah Historical Quarterly* 47.1 (Winter 1979): 42–53.

5   See Gavin Feller, "Sacralising Signals for the Institution and the Individual: KZN and the LDS Church's Approach to Radio as a New Medium," *Culture and Religion* 16.3 (2015): 327–334; Feller, *Eternity in the Ether*, 55–68. For educational context, see Thomas W. Simpson, *American Universities and the Birth of Modern Mormonism, 1867–1940* (Chapel Hill: University of North Carolina Press, 2016). For media context, see Jeffrey Sconce, *Haunted Media: Electronic Presence from Telegraphy to Television* (Durham, NC: Duke University Press, 2000).

6   Pearl F. Jacobson, "Utah's First Radio Station," *Utah Historical Quarterly* 32.2 (Spring 1964): 130–144. President Grant read verses from D&C 76. See also Heber G. Wolsey, "The History of Radio Station KSL from 1922 to Television" (PhD dissertation, Michigan State University, Lansing, 1967); Richard L. Evans, "Commercial Broadcasting with Salt Lake City Applications and Comparisons" (MA thesis, University of Utah, Salt Lake City, 1931).

7   See Sherry Pack Baker and Elizabeth Mott, "From Radio to the Internet: Church Use of Electronic Media in the Twentieth Century," in *A Firm Foundation: Church Organization and Administration*, ed. David J. Whittaker and Arnold K. Garr (Salt Lake City: Deseret Book, 2011), 339–360.

8   See Tim Larson and Craig Wirth, *Earl J. Glade: An Inside Story of Church and State, Politics, and Media* (Salt Lake City: King's English Bookshop, 2019); D. W. Meinig, "The Mormon Culture Region: Strategies and Patterns in the Geography of the American West, 1847–1964," *Annals of the Association of American Geographers* 55.2 (June 1965): 191–219. For a contemporaneous example from the Rio Grande Valley of radio-supported ethnic regionalism, see Leif Sorensen, "Region and Ethnicity on the Air," *MELUS* 41.2 (Summer 2016): 7–26.

9   In 1928, Grant consulted with Harvey Fletcher about installing this system; their correspondence is in the Fletcher Papers, box 2, fd. 1.

10 First Presidency to Presidents of Stakes and Presidents of Missions, March 3, 1930, in James R. Clark, comp., *Messages of the First Presidency*, vol. 5 (Salt Lake City: Bookcraft, 1971), 273–286, quote on 276; see also *One Hundred Years, 1830–1930* (Salt Lake City: Heber J. Grant, 1930).

11 Earl J. Glade Jr., interviewed by Tim Larson, June 24, 1986, Everett L. Cooley Oral History Project, Marriott Library, University of Utah, Salt Lake City, 5.

12 "Tabernacle Choir Sets Record in Broadcasting," *Salt Lake Tribune*, December 16, 1934, 5.

13 I listened to a selection of broadcasts, at five-year intervals, through the Church History Library (CHL) website, by special arrangement. In the 1960s, Evans re-recorded nearly 2,000 of his sermonettes on audiotapes for syndication. Posthumously, these tapes became the property of his family, who continued to mail batches of them to KMOX, 1120 AM, St. Louis, Missouri, which aired *Richard Evans's Thought for the Day* every weekday morning at 6:55 until June 1998—and then for a brief time longer made the soothing voice available to loyal listeners by phone line. Evans continued to receive fan mail at the Gateway to the West a generation after his death. Only Jack Buck, voice of the St. Louis Cardinals, had a longer tenure on KMOX. See "The Thought for Today . . . and Evermore," *St. Louis Post-Dispatch*, December 10, 1996; "Richard L. Evans Is an Eternal Presence on KMOX Radio," *Wall Street Journal*, February 24, 1997. To stream these sermonettes, go to richardlevans.org.

14 Details from Roscoe A. Grover, interviewed by Gordon Irving, February–March 1979, OH 434, CHL. For context, see Paddy Scannell and David Cardiff, *A Social History of British Broadcasting*, vol. 1: *1922–1939: Serving the Nation* (Oxford: Blackwell, 1991); Frances Dyson, "The Genealogy of the Radio Voice," in *Radio Rethink: Art, Sound, and Transmission*, ed. Daina Augaitis and Dan Lander (Banff, AB: Walter Phillips Gallery, 1994), 167–186.

15 See Allison McCracken, *Real Men Don't Sing: Crooning in American Culture* (Durham, NC: Duke University Press, 2015).

16 Edward P. Kimball, "A Reprehensible Practice," *Improvement Era* 35.8 (June 1932): 490.

17 Lip groove detail from Jonice L. Hubbard, "Pioneers in Twentieth Century Mormon Media: Oral Histories of Latter-day Saint Electronic and Public Relations Professionals" (MA thesis, Brigham Young University, Provo, 2007), 57.

18 See Jessie L. Embry, "'New Ways of Proselyting': Radio and Missionary Work in the 1930s," in *Go Ye into All the World: The Growth and Development of Mormon Missionary Work*, ed. Reid L. Neilson and Fred E. Woods (Salt Lake City: Deseret Book, 2012), 117–150. I also consulted "Eastern States Mission manuscript history and historical reports, 1830–1977," LR 2475-2, CHL.

19 "Roscoe A. Grover papers, 1935–1938," MS 6479, fd. 7, CHL.

20 "Roscoe A. Grover papers," fd. 7. On and off the radio, music missionaries were not uncommon in this period—for example, the Millennial Chorus (1936–1939) in the British Mission, the Traveling Elders (1947–1951) in the Argentine Mission, and the Mormonaires (1951–1952) in the North Central States Mission. Likewise, the "missionary quartet," an LDS version of the barbershop quartet, was a feature of church and even Tabernacle performances into the 1950s.

21 Sheri L. Dew, *Go Forward with Faith: The Biography of Gordon B. Hinckley* (Salt Lake City: Deseret Book, 1996), 93. See also Matthew Porter Wilcox, "The Resources and Results of the Radio, Publicity, and Mission Literature Committee, 1935–1942" (MA thesis, Brigham Young University, Provo, 2013). James B. Keysor owned the local business that pressed the "missionary records" for the Church in the 1940s and 1950s.

22   See Terryl Givens, *The Viper on the Hearth: Mormons, Myths, and the Construction of Heresy* (New York: Oxford University Press, 1997); Fluhman, *A Peculiar People*; Megan Sanborn Jones, *Performing American Identity in Anti-Mormon Melodrama* (London: Routledge, 2009).

23   This paragraph, and this chapter, is informed by "Radio, Publicity, and Mission Literature Committee Executive Secretary Files, 1938–1952," CR 21-1, CHL; "Council of the Twelve Apostles chairman files, 1935–1943," CR 21-5, CHL; "Radio, Publicity, and Mission Literature Committee miscellaneous documents, circa 1935–1950," CR 21-14, CHL.

24   See Hal Erickson, *Religious Radio and Television in the United States, 1921–1991: The Programs and Personalities* (Jefferson, NC: McFarland, 1992); Thomas F. X. Hoar, "Religious Broadcasting, 1920–1980: Four Religious Broadcast Pioneers and the Process of Evangelization" (PhD dissertation, Salve Regina University, Newport, RI, 2011); Michael E. Pohlman, "Broadcasting the Faith: Protestant Religious Radio and Theology in America, 1920–1950" (PhD dissertation, Southern Baptist Theological Seminary, Louisville, KY, 2011); Heather Hendershot, *What's Fair on the Air? Cold War Right-Wing Broadcasting and the Public Interest* (Chicago: University of Chicago Press, 2011); David A. Noell, "Broadcasting Faith: Regulating Radio from the New Era to the American Century" (PhD dissertation, Columbia University, New York City, 2020); Tona J. Hangen, *Redeeming the Dial: Radio, Religion, and Popular Culture in America* (Chapel Hill: University of North Carolina Press, 2022).

25   I listened to this and other now-digitized sound files from "Church of the Air audio recordings, 1937–1969," AV 221, CHL.

26   Heber J. Grant, untitled talk, October 3, 1941, in *One Hundred Twelfth Semi-annual Conference* (Salt Lake City: LDS Church, 1941), 6. The audio recording of this session has been digitized by the CHL. For biographical context, see Ronald W. Walker, *Qualities That Count: Heber J. Grant as Businessman, Missionary, and Apostle* (Provo: Brigham Young University Press, 2004). For the sonic dimension of disability studies, see Jonathan Sterne, *Diminished Faculties: A Political Phenomenology of Impairment* (Durham, NC: Duke University Press, 2021).

27   Roscoe A. Grover interview, 36.

28   *The Diaries of J. Reuben Clark, 1931–1961, Abridged* (Salt Lake City: n.p., 2010), 11–12, entries for February 11, 1934, and March 4, 1934.

29   *Diaries of J. Reuben Clark*, 18.

30   J. Russell Scott, interviewed by Don Ripplinger, June 17, 1992, CR 352-347, 42, CHL.

31   These titles from Harper were *Unto the Hills* (1940), *This Day . . . and Always* (1942), *. . . and "The Spoken Word"* (1943), *At This Same Hour* (1945), *From within These Walls* (1946), *Tonic for Our Times* (1952), *From the Crossroads* (1955), *The Everlasting Things* (1957), *May Peace Be with You* (1961), and *Faith in the Future* (1963). These were followed by other regionally published quotebooks—Mormon "Chicken Soup for the Soul," to use a corporate anachronism. Unfortunately, I was not able to peruse Richard L. Evans's papers at the CHL, not even the fan letters, for the entire collection is restricted.

32   Evelyn Bigsby, "The Spoken Word by Richard Evans," *TV-Radio Life*, May 27, 1956, 50.

33   "Milestones," *Time* 98.20 (November 15, 1971), 53.

34   See Tona J. Hangen, *Redeeming the Dial: Radio, Religion, and Popular Culture in America* (Chapel Hill: University of North Carolina Press, 2002); Timothy H. Sherwood, *The Rhetorical Leadership of Fulton J. Sheen, Norman Vincent Peale, and Billy Graham in the Age of Extremes* (Lanham, MD: Lexington Books, 2013); Kirk D. Farney, *Ministers of a New Medium: Broadcasting Theology in the Radio Ministries of Fulton J. Sheen and Walter A. Maier* (Westmont, IL: InterVarsity Press, 2022); J. Inscoe, "Sonic Waves of Grain: Paul Harvey's American Evangelism" (PhD dissertation, University of Maryland, Baltimore County, 2021); Isaac Weiner, *Religion Out Loud: Religious Sound, Public Space, and American Pluralism* (New York: New York University Press, 2013).

35   See Eric A. Eliason, *The J. Golden Kimball Stories* (Urbana: University of Illinois Press, 2007).

36   See David G. Pace, "Maud May Babcock: Speak Clearly and Carry a Big Umbrella," in *Worth Their Salt: Notable but Often Unnoted Women of Utah*, ed. Colleen Whitley (Logan: Utah State University Press, 1996), 148–157; for context, Martha Sonntag Bradley-Evans, "Women in the Arts: Evolving Roles and Diverse Expressions," in *Women in Utah History: Paradigm or Paradox?* ed. Linda Thatcher and Patricia Lyn Scott (Logan: Utah State University Press, 2005), 324–359. Another qualified woman was Irma May Felt Bitner (1888–1965), mother of five and manager of the KSL artist bureau, who cast and coached the station's radio players.

5

MUSICAL ACTIVITY

Babcock was one member of a vast cultural apparatus that existed in Mormondom from the 1920s through the 1960s. During the post-Manifesto transformation of the religion, the Church subtracted polygyny (erstwhile "the principle") as well as the temple oath of vengeance, and it demoted female ritual healing, glossolalia, charisma, and apocalypticism. On the plus side of the ledger, Mormonism added bureaucracy, Americanism, institutional racism, teetotalism, and "activity." An "active" Utah Mormon of the 1920s notionally took the sacrament every Sunday and visited a temple at least once a year. However, religious attendance was not yet central to religious identity, and "activity" could be fulfilled in other ways, including attendance at meetings and events sponsored by the Church's five "auxiliaries." Each of these—the children's Primary, the Young Men's Mutual Improvement Association (MIA), the Young Women's MIA, the women's Relief Society, and the Deseret Sunday School Union—sponsored volunteer performing groups, especially choirs. Volunteerism became constitutive of the faith. Back when Mormonism was a western regional ethnicity, that ethnicity was performed in public.[1]

Three pillars supported LDS singing at the ward and stake (diocese) levels. First, the Salt Lake Tabernacle Choir provided a model and an inspiration. Second, the Church Music Committee (1920–1969) issued guidelines, published textbooks, and codified the hymnal and other songsters. Third, the McCune School of Music (1924–1957), a Church-owned lyceum in a red-rock mansion on Salt Lake City's Capitol Hill, offered subsidized in-person master classes for organists and choristers on the Wasatch Front; for hinterland Mormons, the school sent prominent musicians—many of them trained at the New England Conservatory of

https://doi.org/10.5876/781646427031.c005

Music—on the road to give workshops, something like extension agents of agricultural colleges.[2]

One person, Tracy Y. Cannon, made his imprint on the committee and the school as the long-term director of both. Born in 1879, Cannon joined the Salt Lake Tabernacle Choir at age fifteen. He studied organ under John J. McClellan and in 1909 became an assistant organist in the Tabernacle. The year before, at age twenty, he received his patriarchal blessing, which included these acoustical instructions: "Listen also in obedience to the whisperings of that Still Small Voice which cometh from our Father in Heaven." The Presiding Patriarch, John Smith, nephew of the Prophet, continued: "It shall be thy privilege to guide and direct, to teach and to ex[h]ort . . . Thy voice shall be heard among the nations of the earth and shall be an instrument in the hand of the Lord."[3] As an old man, Cannon recorded for posterity that he had, as a young man, followed this auditory counsel: "I developed a keen realization of the need of improving our Church music and the spirit of prophecy whispered to me that some day I would be in a high positional musically in the Church."[4]

In one of its earliest memos, from 1920, the Church Music Committee—a sort of mini-auxiliary—announced its mission using a keyword: "to correlate."[5] This was a corporate management term related to compliance and quality assurance, but it had theological implications in the post-polygyny era, when the essence of Mormonism was up for grabs. Long-bearded president Joseph F. Smith, another nephew of the founder and the final polygamous prophet, had organized the first Correlation Committee in 1912. In the long run, correlation—co-opted by priesthood bureaucrats in the mold of beardless ambassador-turned-apostle J. Reuben Clark—would lead to orthodoxy and orthopraxy, a standardization of religious belief and practice. But correlation originally had other energies and potential outcomes.[6] In reference to music, the correlating impulse was related to Progressivism—that is, societal uplift through efficient application of professional expertise. The committee's trained musicians hoped to oversee a grand unification of community music making. Its motto— "variety of expression, but unity of purpose"—denoted a kind of practical theology in which activity and artistry existed in harmonious counterpoint.

In addition to greater standardization of education, repertoire, and programming, the committee sought a higher standard of musicianship.

One of the signal products of musical correlation was a trio of Church-published music books to replace the former array of psalmodies and songsters. After the arrival of *Hymns* (1948/1950), *Recreational Songs* (1949), and *The Children Sing* (1951), ward members everywhere could practice the same songs. Much as the Church Music Committee in Salt Lake set universal standards, each individual Ward Music Committee was supposed to "correlate" all local-level music units, making sure auxiliaries planned together to create a regular and full calendar of performances as well as executing a program for improving congregational singing. In this era, many Latter-day Saints went to chapel multiple times during the work week—not counting twice on Sundays—because each auxiliary held its own meetings. And each of those ward gatherings included congregational singing. This is why Cannon believed a properly functioning ward required six organists plus six choristers. To turn that ideal into reality, more than 10 percent of the adults in a typical ward (~100 participating adults) would need to accept music leadership callings.[7]

Cannon had no power but the imprimatur of the First Presidency, but that was in fact a measure of power in a culture increasingly defined by compliance with priesthood directives. Ironically or not, the obedient production of community events during the "ward culture climax" relied disproportionately on women. Many small-town bishops (lay pastors) neglected to return Cannon's incessant questionnaires and failed to organize choirs. But in many wards and stakes, Relief Society women picked up the slack and made things happen. They enjoyed considerable autonomy in their local execution of directives from Salt Lake.[8]

For Cannon, making music for activity's sake wasn't enough. He wanted excellence; he wanted the "super-fine." He considered the development of musical talents—gifts from God—a sacred duty. He hoped to nurture future LDS composers while developing Church-wide literacy in the canon of European classical music. Elder Cannon set nearly utopian goals for amateurs performing music in rural locales. In 1943, he convinced the First Presidency to approve a nomenclatural change that expressed these ambitions: the Ward Music Committee became the "Ward Music Guild." Guild members had the task of improving the quality of music, of dignifying the work of choristers and organists, and of ensuring the smooth scheduling of music for annual events: the Primary conference, the Primary festival, the MIA opera, an Easter cantata, the Priesthood anniversary, and the ward bazaar (a fundraiser).

"Where there is good music leadership, there is good music" was Cannon's personal motto. "Good" connoted musicianship—and propriety. The Church Music Committee had conservative tastes. It stipulated that hymns should always be sung at moderate tempos. It strongly preferred that every ward have a pipe organ, not an electronic one. Organ was invariably the best instrument; piano was conditionally appropriate; brass and percussion were suspect. Outdoors, at social gatherings, Latter-day Saints had license to sing a wide variety of "folk music," including spirituals, as collected in *Recreational Songs*; but the chapel was reserved for *Hymns* and select works of the "masters" (e.g., Handel and Haydn). No evangelical pop songs and no Black spirituals were permitted inside its walls.[9]

Compared to most low-level bureaucrats in the history of bureaucracy, Cannon had reason to feel good about his large-scale impact. He could walk from his conservatory office—draped in wine-colored silk and adorned with a full-size marble statue of Cleopatra as well as a bust of Richard Wagner—down the hill to the Salt Lake Tabernacle to see evidence of his success: events like the back-to-back costumed performances of Mendelssohn's *Elijah* on the Saturday evening of October General Conference in 1938 and 1939, which included an MIA cast of hundreds. Similar large-scale ticketed concerts by LDS amateurs in the Tabernacle became regular features: Mendelssohn's *St. Paul*, "massed ward choir" festivals, the Pioneer Centennial Pageant in 1947, and four consecutive Easter Sunday performances of *A German Requiem* (sung in English) in the years 1949–1952.[10]

Meanwhile, the Relief Society—the most powerful of the auxiliaries and the most independent—sponsored its own choirs whose members sang from its own songbook and consulted advice on singing and conducting from its own magazine. "A singing Mother makes a happy home," said Relief Society president Louise Y. Robison.[11] Whether you lived in Bannock, Idaho, or Beaver, Utah, to join a group of "Singing Mothers" required memorization of standard selections (including Schubert, Mendelssohn, and Rossini) according to stipulated tempo, intonation, phrasing, enunciation, and pronunciation. Confederated groups of Singing Mothers had a separate annual repertoire—for example, Gounod and Grieg plus a mountain home composer. As arranged by Robison, one of these augmented choirs—250 strong in handmade uniforms of white blouses and black skirts—sang over the radio from the Tabernacle to the Hall of Science at Chicago's Century of Progress Exposition, where the International Congress of Women met in July 1933. With Charlotte (Lottie) Owens Sackett as conductor, Singing Mothers also appeared at the 1964 world's fair in Queens, New York; put on original pageants; performed on KSL; released albums; helped dedicated the Hyde Park (London) Temple at the request of the First Presidency; and regularly sang in General Conference, including primetime weekend sessions, from the 1930s through the 1950s.[12]

The MIA, too, had a separate music committee; LDS composer Crawford Gates (best known for the Pioneer Centennial musical *Promised Valley*) was a long-term member. During its glory years in the 1950s and 1960s, the MIA sponsored "road shows," musical comedies, and all-Church music and dance festivals that filled venues like the Hollywood Bowl and the football stadium at the University of Utah. With clearer vision than Cannon, Gates and his colleagues recognized the tension that existed between the professional class and the laity. Not all wards had the same capacity: some had more members, bigger budgets, and greater musical talent and training. The MIA committee drew a distinction between the "powerhouse wards" of the Wasatch Front and the average "Podunk ward" in the intermountain "middle of nowhere."[13] The committee wanted both types of congregations to stage festivals every June, using the same correlated programs, so it provided simplified arrangements for smaller ensembles in the hinterland.

My maternal grandmother belonged to one of those Podunk wards, in Georgetown, Idaho (Bear Lake County), which had a population of ±500 in the 1940s–1960s. In her diary, alongside a record of endless domestic labor, Lela Willett Clark noted an astonishing amount of communal music: a yearly Easter cantata at the stake tabernacle in Montpelier; a yearly Christmas cantata at the high school, also in Montpelier; spring music festivals in the village; grade school, high school, and MIA operettas; a touring operetta from a ward in Idaho Falls; pageants organized by the local Primary, MIA, and Relief Society; a pageant at the Logan Temple; and a Logan performance of *Oratorio from the Book of Mormon* by Leroy Robertson, a member of the Church Music Committee.[14]

Throughout the rural US in the days of the Great Depression and World War II, before fast cars and smooth freeways, and before television, people had to entertain themselves. Typically, they did so at church, at school, or in the roadhouse. Latter-day Saints didn't drink—at least not anymore; the Word of Wisdom became mandatory in this period—which removed one of the three venues. In the post-polygyny era, Latter-day Saints turned activity into identity at church-like schools and school-like ward buildings. Musical performance constituted a sphere of special pride given that the Church—a historic object of hostility and scorn—had achieved its most notable PR victories through the Tabernacle Organ and Choir. Every Sunday morning, active ward members could tune into KSL, 1160 AM, to hear their ensign bearers before leaving their houses for the chapel, their second home.

NOTES

1   For context, see Patricia Nelson Limerick, "Peace Initiative: Using the Mormons to Rethink Culture and Ethnicity in American History," *Journal of Mormon History* 21.2 (Fall 1995): 1–29; Thomas G. Alexander, "Church Administrative Change in the Progressive Period, 1898–1930," in Whittaker and Garr, eds., *A Firm Foundation*, 295–317.

2   This built on the practice of LDS "art missions" to Paris; see Martha Elizabeth Bradley and Lowell M. Durham Jr., "John Hafen and the Art Missionaries," *Journal of Mormon History* 12 (1985): 91–105; Linda Jones Gibbs, *Harvesting the Light: The Paris Art Mission and Beginnings of Utah Impressionism* (Salt Lake City: The Church of Jesus Christ of Latter-day Saints, 1987); Heather Belnap, "Mormon/Latter-day Saint Art," in *Variations in Christian Art: Mennonite, Mormon, Quaker, and Swedenborgian*, ed. Diane Apostolos-Cappadona (London: Bloomsbury, 2024), 77–168.

3   Patriarchal blessing by John Smith, September 1, 1899, in "Tracy Y. Cannon Papers, 1899–1961," MS 14557, Church History Library (CHL), Salt Lake City, UT.

4   "How I Became a Musician," n.d., in Caroline Hinckley Cannon, comp., "Tracy Y. Cannon: His Life and His Legacy" (1979), MS 14555, CHL

5   Melvin J. Ballard, chairman, to the Stake Presidency, December 14, 1920, "Music Department circular letters," CR 108-3, box 1, fd. 1, CHL.

6   See especially Matthew Bowman, "Zion: The Progressive Roots of Mormon Correlation," in *Directions for Mormon Studies in the Twenty-first Century*, ed. Patrick Q. Mason (Salt Lake City: University of Utah Press, 2016), 15–34.

7   On the past LDS music education system, see Eldon D. Brinley, "The Recreational Life of the Mormon People" (ED dissertation, New York University, New York City, 1943); Conrad B. Harrison, "The Role of Music in the Mormon Church," *Music Journal* 2.6 (January 1, 1944): 6–7, 42; Harold Laycock, "Music Education in the Church of Jesus Christ of Latter-day Saints," *BYU Studies* 4.2 (Winter 1962): 107–118; Jay L. Slaughter, "The Role of Music in the Mormon Church, School, and Life" (PhD dissertation, Indiana University, Bloomington, 1964); Verena Ursenbach, *Worship and Music in the Church of Jesus Christ of Latter-day Saints* (self-published, 1968); Grant L. Anderson, "Some Educational Aspects of the Music Training Program of the Church of Jesus Christ of Latter-day Saints, 1935–1969" (MA thesis, Brigham Young University, Provo, 1976); Ardis E. Parshall, "You Have Been Listening to 'Latter-day Saint Music,' 1937," https://keepapitchinin.org/2015/08/14/you-have-been-listening-to-latter-day-saint -music-1937.

8   See Colleen McDannell, "Mormon Gender in the Mid-Twentieth Century," in *The Routledge Handbook of Mormonism and Gender*, ed. Amy Hoyt and Taylor G. Petrey (London: Routledge, 2020), 143–156; Jill Mulvay Derr, Janath Russell Cannon, and Maureen Ursenbach Beecher, *Women of Covenant: The Story of Relief Society* (Salt Lake City: Deseret Book, 1992), 304–340.

9   This paragraph, and this chapter, draws from my perusal of "Music Department subject and correspondence files, 1919–1973," CR 108-10, boxes 1, 3–5, 10, and 12, CHL.

10   Musical and technical conditions in mid-twentieth-century Salt Lake City allowed Maurice Abravanel, conductor of the Utah Symphony, to make the first studio and first stereo recording of Mahler's Eighth, the "Symphony of a Thousand," beating out Leonard Bernstein and Eugene Ormandy, who lacked ready access to the necessary choral capacity in New York and Philadelphia, respectively. The Salt Lake Tabernacle served as the stereophonic studio for the Vanguard LP, released in 1964.

11   Quoted in Derr, Cannon, and Beecher, *Women of Covenant*, 273.

12   Unfortunately, few secondary sources on the Singing Mothers exist; start with Annie Wells Cannon, "The Relief Society Singing Mothers," *Improvement Era* 42.3 (March 1939): 154–155, 162.

13   Crawford M. Gates, interviewed by Gordon Irving, 1985–1990, OH 961, 115, CHL. Choral festivals seem to have been dominated by young women, who, unlike young men, did not have the option of Church-affiliated scouting and Church-sponsored basketball tournaments, which were organized in the same scalar fashion (ward/stake/area), leading to an "all-Church championship." See Jessie L. Embry, "'Spiritualized Recreation': LDS All-Church Athletic Tournaments, 1950–1971," *BYU Studies* 48.3 (2009): 93–124.

14   See Owen E. Clark and Barbara S. Clark, eds., *Diary of Lela W. Clark*, vol. 1 (self-published, 2022), available at Amazon.com/Diary-Lela-W-Clark-Story/dp /B0BJF419BW. For context, see Lowry Nelson, *The Mormon Village, a Pattern and Technique of Land Settlement* (Salt Lake City: University of Utah Press, 1952); Douglas D. Alder, "The Mormon Ward: Congregation or Community?" *Journal of Mormon History* 5 (1978): 61–78; Jessie L. Embry, *Mormon Wards as Community* (Binghamton, NY: Binghamton University, 2001).

6

MOTAB SOUND

In 1935, Heber J. Grant tapped J. Spencer Cornwall, superintendent of music for the public schools of Salt Lake City, to be the Tabernacle's next music director. Cornwall's conducting career had begun two decades before, with a local glee club that performed in blackface in a tent by Parleys Creek, singing minstrel songs to raise money to erect an LDS chapel. The shtick of the "Richards Ward Male Chorus" became so popular that the club changed its name to the "Swanee Singers." No matter that anti-Mormons had previously mocked Latter-day Saints with anti-Black songs such as "The Mormon Coon" (released on a 78-rpm phonographic record by Victor Talking Machine in 1905); for white people, the appeal of racist entertainment transcended religious difference. In its respectable "whiteface" mode, the Swanee Singers performed at Temple Square multiple times, including General Conference sessions.[1]

As soon as he inherited the flagship weekly radio program, Cornwall encountered a structural problem: there was no way for the conductor to know what the choir sounded like on air, since each performance was broadcast live. Within a year or two, a KSL technician told Cornwall he could make an electrical transcription off the line. When Cornwall listened to the disc—"Worthy Is the Lamb" from *Messiah*—he was dismayed to hear a blast of static, then the faintest pianissimo. "The result was thoroughly ludicrous, and everyone laughed," he recalled. "I was stunned."[2] The engineer in charge of the broadcast explained that he had been afraid that the choir would blow out the vacuum tubes on the signal generator, so he decreased the input before realizing he had gone too far. "It was providential that listeners in those early days of broadcasting were more concerned in getting distance than quality," Cornwall later remarked.[3]

https://doi.org/10.5876/781646427031.c006

With the approval of J. Reuben Clark, the Church upgraded the Tabernacle so that a technician could be onsite for every rehearsal and broadcast. A control booth had to be designed and built in a manner that did not mar the symmetry of the building's interior. By fall 1938, the booth was up and running, including a sound-mixing console and a transcription disc recorder. This "third ear" allowed Cornwall to listen to rehearsals more or less as they would sound on the radio.[4] He made adjustments as necessary—to his conducting and also to his instructions to the technician, who mixed the sound on Sundays, following a marked score. The pickup system grew from one microphone on a stand to sixteen mikes strategically installed on wires above the loft. The placement and fine-tuning were done over ten long days by none other than Harvey Fletcher of Bell Labs, who asked the choir to sing short phrases again and again as he performed his electronic adjustments. The effort resulted in a "great upsurge of fan letters."[5] All the new equipment had an additional benefit: the Church could now record its own sixteen-inch discs for missionary radio use.

In a second round of improvements, KSL engineers C. Richard (Dick) Evans and Stanley D. Rees addressed the old problem of sound lag from the organ, which made the choir go flat. Instead of using a string quartet or a pump organ, Cornwall accepted the idea of an electronic pitch-correcting system. Technicians placed three large speakers on stands below the choir. This equipment allowed the singers to hear the amplified organ instantaneously, ever so slightly before they heard the same pipes acoustically. After one of these heavy loudspeakers fell on a child sitting in the front row, the Church authorized an expensive upgrade: roughly sixty small Western Electric speakers installed under the choir's seats. When the singers went flat, the volume of these speakers could be increased from the booth. Eventually, an amplifier knob was added to the conductor's stand. The job of turning the knob fell to J. Russell Scott, a choir member with perfect pitch.

Cornwall remembered the first broadcast after the pitch-correction system was working properly: "That's the most wonderful *Word* I've ever heard. They're all on. They're tuned."[6] The choir could only be "tuned" electronically if it were "in tune" with the signal, which was different than being attuned to the sound. In an oral history, Scott described the system as subliminal. The choir does not hear the organ through the speakers per se, said Scott; rather, these subtle pools of electronic sounds have an unconscious effect on tuning, and the singers come up in pitch. They are "sensitive to it," he remarked. "They don't realize they're hearing it but it is there and they begin to react to it."[7] He might well have been describing the still small voice—words of the spirit one feels more than hears.

Over thousands of rehearsals and broadcasts and with just as many adjustments and improvements to mikes and mixing boards, the peculiar acoustics of the Salt Lake Tabernacle—originally thought impossible for recording—became legible to technicians. In the process, this idiosyncratic nineteenth-century edifice became the Radio City Music Hall of Mormondom. Perhaps no other auditorium has ever been used so often as a recording studio. "Early radio demanded dampened, draped studios to avoid feedback," recalled Cornwall. "But as technology improved, allowing for wider range of frequencies, sound engineers wanted more brilliant sound," or "liveness."[8] The studio known as the Tabernacle abounded in that quality, so building managers removed the curtains that had formerly been lowered during broadcasts. With each passing year, KSL technicians got closer to the elusive goal of fidelity in five dimensions: choral balance, reproduction of low tones, balance between organ and choir, clear diction, and desirable presence (sense of intimacy). There remained, however, the persistent problem of broadcasting dynamic contrasts—shifts from loud to soft or soft to loud. To compensate, the choir under Cornwall learned to repress dynamic extremes; this repression became part of its signature sound, a perfect complement to Richard Evans's un-harsh voice.

Experimentally, Mormons could be forced to be loud. In early 1940, Fletcher returned to Salt Lake City to make a special recording of the Tabernacle Choir and Organ in three-channel stereophonic sound, which he had recently invented. The selections included a Bach prelude, a Widor toccata, and "Come, Come, Ye Saints."[9] To demonstrate his attainment of "high fidelity," Bell Labs held a demonstration in Carnegie Hall—an acousmatic concert without performers that recalled spiritualist seances of the nineteenth century. To the surprise of the Manhattan audience, the stage contained nothing but a trinity of speakers. Leopold Stokowski, celebrity conductor of the Philadelphia Orchestra, was ceremoniously given control of the mixing board. When he got to the choir's recording of Elijah's appeal to the Lord (from the oratorio by Mendelssohn), the maestro "enhanced" the sound "until it sounded like a million banshees wailing at once," which caused the crowd to shout spontaneously. Previously, at a rehearsal of this demonstration, a woman "doubled up as if kicked by a horse," reported the *New York Herald Tribune*.[10] This was possibly the first time since the dedication of the Kirtland Temple—the Mormon Pentecost—that Latter-day Saints attained an Old Testament sound: the noise of many waters.

For its radio program, the choir never sang fortissimo, which would have obscured the lyrics. Cornwall was a stickler for enunciation; he wanted listeners to understand the sung word as well as the spoken word. He had a list of rules printed on cardstock "to be read twice weekly until memorized." In addition to knowing the difference between lip consonants and tongue consonants, dutiful choir members showed up early so microphones could be adjusted properly. Cornwall's list ended in boldface: "**Do remember that the ears of all nations are listening to you.**"[11] These ears were more important than those of the live audience. Appropriately, the radio show had greater fidelity in a partially empty Tabernacle. Harvey Fletcher's mentee Vern Knudsen—another LDS physicist and another founding member of the Acoustical Society of America—eventually quantified the optimal audience size for moderating the reverberation: 2,500 people.[12]

The combination of comprehensible singing and plain speaking struck a chord nationally. With the advent of World War II, the US finally reciprocated the LDS Church's post-Manifesto embrace of Americanism. In 1944, the United States Army Radio network added *Music and the Spoken Word* to its lineup. Troops stationed stateside heard it live; troops in England, Hawai'i, and Australia heard it on delay by means of a transcription disc. (The KSL signal was so strong that Navy men in the South Pacific sometimes heard it live, too.) Also in 1944, the United States Department of War asked the choir to contribute to the soundtrack for the Allied propaganda film *The Battle of San Pietro*. A religion once deemed a threat to democracy could now sing against fascism. In the emergent "Judeo-Christian" conception of "tri-faith America," Latter-day Saints became honorary members of the Protestant third. "Zion has exchanged her horns for the American Dream," wrote LDS-born novelist Maurine Whipple in 1945.[13]

A key moment in the convergence of nationalism and LDS music making came on April 12 of that year, when Franklin Delano Roosevelt passed away in Warm Springs, Georgia, at 3:35 p.m. As luck would have it, he died on a Thursday, one of the choir's regular rehearsal days. Knowing this, CBS called the Church and asked if Cornwall and Evans could perform that evening. In a show of Mormon industry and organization, they pulled it off. Evans's reassuring voice eulogized the man who had changed the norms of presidential speech by talking conversationally from his fireside directly to citizens' homes.[14] CBS broadcast this memorial music and the spoken word over its entire network—140 stations, about double the choir's usual audience. Among other selections, it sang "Lacrimosa" from Mozart's *Requiem*.[15]

After World War II, US companies redirected much of the mighty engine of war production to consumer goods, including recorded music. CBS had plans for the Mormons. In 1948, Columbia Records, a division of CBS, unveiled a twelve-inch long-playing disc that could hold twenty minutes per side at 33 rpm. The following year, to mark the twentieth anniversary of *Music and the Spoken Word*, CBS/Columbia made a double album of the choir as a token of gratitude. For the anniversary broadcast in July 1949, CBS president Frank Stanton came to Utah to do some of the speaking to an audience estimated at 10 million.

The quarter-century mark—the conventional duration of a "generation" —brought even higher accolades. *Life* magazine hailed the weekly program as a "national institution" and a "great chord of common thoughts."[16] President Dwight D. Eisenhower and former president Herbert Hoover sent congratulations. For the silver jubilee broadcast, Cornwall led masterworks by Handel and Mendelssohn, Alexander Schreiner played Bach, and Evans shared an unusually personal message about the passage of time and the timelessness of truth. "Not infrequently someone will write, 'I have been listening to you all my life'; and now another generation is listening," he began. The voice of the Tabernacle spoke about the sacred privilege and solemn responsibility of entering another's man's home, for verily, he and fellow broadcasters were accountable for the impact of their utterances on others—whether written or spoken or sung or suggested. Using the intimacy of mass communication, Evans addressed each listener directly: "Thank you for welcoming us in."[17]

At this point, Evans had presided over nearly 1,300 consecutive shows of the "traditional broadcast," writing and delivering every sermonette himself, all while serving as producer. During the 1940s, his voice had become fuller and slower, with longer pauses—still very much a radio cadence but with a hint of portentousness that marked him as an inspirational speaker. He had settled on signature phrases that would henceforth be broadcast from the Tabernacle on Sunday mornings. "Once more we welcome you within these walls with music and the spoken word from the Crossroads of the West," his baritone began. It concluded: "Once more we leave you within the shadows of the everlasting hills. May peace be with you, this day and always."

As the choir grew more famous thanks to CBS/Columbia, it gained more airtime at the expense of the organ, until the radio program reached what Cornwall called the "concordant triad": eighteen minutes of singing, eight minutes of solo keyboard, and three minutes of Evans intoning over soft pipes. The organist—Schreiner or his bitter rival on rotation, Frank W. Asper—soloed with hymn tunes, flashy French toccatas, and pieces that showed off the carillon, chimes, and celesta stops. For choral pieces, Cornwall liked to program Bach to inspire his amateurs to reach the highest level, even though David O. McKay was known to complain about Bach.[18] In general, though, the Church tried to make CBS and its consumer audience happy. Using a spreadsheet, LDS publicity officers analyzed a large sample of fan letters to develop an "over-all formula" for the music selections, wrote Cornwall. The answer "loomed up in the one word *variety*."[19]

Legally speaking, *Music and the Spoken Word* was not a regular radio show with commercial sponsorship and advertisements. Instead, it was a public-service "sustaining program" or "sustainer." Listeners *never* heard "this program was brought to you by The Church of Jesus Christ of Latter-day Saints." Nothing explicitly denominational was allowed to be spoken, according to the rules governing free airtime. However, because Evans generally identified his location as the *Mormon* Tabernacle in Salt Lake City, the LDS Church (and the State of Utah) got free publicity while CBS got free content. In the long run, this mutualism deepened: the national network used *Music and the Spoken Word* as an implicit sales pitch for the choir's LPs on Columbia, the profits from which the choir used as subventions for its tours. In more ways than one, Evans was a voice of subliminal advertising.

In 1951, the LDS Church faced a critical media decision: to refuse or accept the commercial dictate from CBS to run radio advertisements for alcohol and tobacco—two vices expressly prohibited by revelation. In a special meeting with the Quorum of the Twelve Apostles, J. Reuben Clark warned that refusal would relegate KSL to a second- or third-tier station; he wanted to maintain a "dominant" station. Evans agreed: without the "potency" of KSL within the CBS network, the choir's national reach through *Music and the Spoken Word* would be in jeopardy, given the latent prejudices against Latter-day Saints in many large markets. "We are in a practical world and we have to face the thing as it comes," said Clark. His voice carried the day; by apostolic vote, the Church-owned station ran jingles for beer.[20]

With media mammon, the Mormons did their best to advance the Lord's media work. In 1954, President McKay determined that the first stage of the choir's missionary effort—to dispel prejudice—had been accomplished; the second stage, musical proselytizing, could thus commence. This happened in conjunction with McKay's most important decisions as Church president: to modernize the missionary program, to instruct converts to "gather" in their own homelands, to formally end the policy of American Zionism (a development decades in the making), and to build temples overseas—all toward the goal of becoming a worldwide religion. "The Lord has given us the means of whispering through space," said the prophet at a special meeting in the Tabernacle, where he outlined the new missionary program with the help of a motion picture.[21]

The following year, the choir went on tour to Britain and Europe, including West Berlin, where it recorded for Radio Free Europe. The standard tour program was essentially an extended version of *Music and the Spoken Word*, with Richard Evans speaking between numbers. European critics who were expecting a concert from "America's Most Famous Choir" were puzzled by this format and the "motley" program, but the Church considered the tour a resounding success, aided by the traveling pitch-correcting loudspeaker system. McKay authorized a follow-up "Grand American Tour" in 1958, under new music director Richard P. Condie. US audiences, unlike Europeans, expected *Music and the Spoken Word*, and the choir relented to popular demand by playing its theme song each evening, complete with Evans's signature radio phrases in his soft, sociable voice. Unencumbered by Federal Communications Commission rules about religious speech, the concert-hall Evans subtly but methodically interjected gospel doctrine into his performances. He was given billing above the organists, who had been reduced to "accompanists."

The Grand American Tour launched the choir to a new level of fame: it signed a record deal with Eugene Ormandy and the Philadelphia Orchestra; recorded *Messiah*; sang at the White House; performed on Ed Sullivan; broadcast *Music and the Spoken Word* from the Shrine Auditorium in Los Angeles; accepted a Grammy for Best Performance by a Vocal Group or Chorus in the first year of the award show; appeared on a KSL-TV special of patriotic music and narration that won a Peabody Award; and, to top it off, appeared at the January 1965 inauguration of Lyndon B. Johnson.

Throughout this period, the song the choir sang the most was its Grammy-Award–winning version of "Battle Hymn of the Republic." The single hit #13 on the Billboard Hot 100 in 1959, and jocular members of the choir began referring to their organization as "Dick Condie and His Hot 400." Eugene Ormandy, when first rehearsing the "Battle Hymn" with the choir, had said emphatically, twice: "Isn't this corny."[22] But it was the kind of corn that made millions. Many radio stations began playing it at the top of each hour, twenty-four times a day. (The choir sneaked in some proselytization on the B side: Leroy Robertson's setting of the Lord's Prayer from his *Oratorio from the Book of Mormon*.) For Saints who knew their history, the LDS cooption of the "Battle Hymn" was sweet justice, for the author of the anthem, Unitarian abolitionist Julia Ward Howe, had visited Utah Territory and denounced Mormonism as a tyrannical religion that enslaved women.[23] In the long run, too, it must have been satisfying to LDS partisans that the choir's recording of the anthem outperformed a rival one from 1966, also released by Columbia—sung by Anita Bryant, a co-crusader of Billy Graham and the Southern Baptist Convention, a nemesis of the LDS Church. For a brief moment, the LDS sound of collective restraint bested the evangelical mainstream.

Choir members became sick of singing the "Battle Hymn," but that didn't stop them from profiting from it. They sang it for an international hit movie, a spectacular piece of military-industrial entertainment called *This Is Cinerama*, which included footage from a B-25 flying low over the Crossroads of the West.[24] And they did so again in 1962, when the choir, at the special request of CBS, provided part of the soundtrack to the first intercontinental TV broadcast, live from Mount Rushmore, via the commercial satellite known as Telstar—America's answer to Sputnik. For the first time ever, the choir flew on assignment and completed the roundtrip to and from Rapid City, South Dakota, in one extra-long day so the singers could be back in time to perform in the Tabernacle for a Days of '47 evening pageant. During their short appearance at the Shrine of Democracy, the choir started with Martin Luther's "A Mighty Fortress Is Our God" while NBC announcer Chet Huntley took the role of Richard Evans with a voiceover quotation from Abraham Lincoln. Then, in the closing sequence, the choir finished with the "Battle Hymn" while an airborne camera panned over the Manhattan skyline, ending at the United Nations building.[25]

My grandmother Lela Clark, an unemotional person who kept a daily diary for fifty years while barely recording her feelings, wrote in boldface that day: "**World historical event.**"[26] In reference to Telstar, the *Deseret News* editorialized: "Another star of peace came to brighten the world." "LDS Choir Pioneers in Space" headlined its rival, the *Salt Lake Tribune*.[27] Weeks later, in General Conference, apostle Spencer W. Kimball marveled at how in his lifetime the carrying distance of LDS preaching had expanded exponentially. "From yards to miles to Telstars to planets the human voice may now be carried," he said. "The prophet of God may now be heard in all the world, fulfilling completely the command: 'Go ye into all the world, and preach the gospel to every creature.'"[28]

In retrospect, the year of Telstar, 1962, marked the zenith of LDS soft power—when the interests and the tastes of the Church, the US Cold War state, the commercial media establishment, and America's white ruling class all aligned.[29] *Music and the Spoken Word* appeared on nearly 200 CBS affiliates plus the Armed Forces Radio Network plus Voice of

America. The voice of Mormon America, Richard Evans, would be recognized as "Utah Salesman of the Year" in 1965 and would be named president of Rotary International in 1966. But everything would look different after 1968, a year of student protest, race rebellion, and conservative backlash. A musical harbinger of this cultural and political shakeup was a 1962 instrumental by the UK band the Tornadoes. This wordless song was called "Telstar," and it had been recorded in North London the day before the Tabernacle Choir sang the "Battle Hymn" in South Dakota. The single blasted to the top of the charts on both sides of the Atlantic, becoming the first British rock song to reach #1 on the Billboard Hot 100—the vanguard of the British Invasion that would soon arrive in force.[30]

NOTES

1   The recording of "The Mormon Coon," with Bob Smith on vocals, can be heard through the Internet Archive; the sheet music (words by Raymond A. Brown; music by Henry Clay Smith) can be accessed digitally through the Church History Library (CHL). For context, see "34 Years of Music Service Noted in Prize Scrapbook," *Deseret News*, August 19, 1951; Michael Hicks, "Ministering Minstrels," in *Spencer W. Kimball's Record Collection*, 73–100; Reeve, *Religion of a Different Color*, 171–187.

2   J. Spencer Cornwall, *A Century of Singing: The Salt Lake Mormon Tabernacle Choir* (Salt Lake City: Deseret Book, 1958), 204.

3   J. Spencer Cornwall, interviewed by Carol Cornwall Madsen, October 19–27, 1980, OH 055, 4, CHL.

4   "Choir Records Singing on Rare Machine," *Salt Lake Tribune*, September 4, 1938.

5   Cornwall, *Century of Singing*, 232.

6   J. Spencer Cornwall, interviewed by James D. Maher Jr., May 3, 1975, OH 466, 23, CHL.

7   J. Russell Scott, interviewed by Don Ripplinger, June 17, 1992, CR 352-347, 42, CHL, 36. Cornwall also noted that "temperatures somewhat above the normal (68 to 72 degrees) induce better 'in tune' singing"; *Century of Singing*, 32.

8   *Century of Singing*, 201.

9   "Program of Stereophonic Recordings," March 17, 1940, Fletcher Papers, box 21, fd. 3.

10   "Super-Volume Concert Records Scare Audience," *New York Herald Tribune*, April 10, 1940. See also Robert E. McGinn, "Stokowski and the Bell Telephone Laboratories: Collaboration in the Development of High-Fidelity Sound Reproduction," *Technology and Culture* 24.1 (January 1983): 38–75. Previously, Carnegie Hall had been booked by Thomas A. Edison, Incorporated, for musical "re-creations" or "tone-tests"; see Emily Thompson, "Machines, Music, and the Quest for Fidelity: Marketing the Edison Phonograph in America, 1877–1925," *Musical Quarterly* 79.1 (Spring 1995): 131–171.

11   "Cornwall's Rules," CR 352-11, fd. 11, CHL.

12   Vern O. Knudsen, "Architectural Acoustics," *Scientific American* 209.5 (November 1963): 78–95. See also Sarah Rollins, "The Salt Lake Tabernacle: Acoustic Characterization and Study of Spatial Variation" (MS thesis, Brigham Young University, Provo, 2005).

13   Maurine Whipple, *This Is the Place: Utah* (New York: Alfred A. Knopf, 1945), 214. For context, see Kevin M. Schultz, *Tri-Faith America: How Catholics and Jews Held Postwar America to Its Protestant Promise* (Oxford: Oxford University Press, 2011).

14   See Kathleen Hall Jamieson, *Eloquence in an Electronic Age: The Transformation of Political Speechmaking* (New York: Oxford University Press, 1990).

15   This paragraph, and the remainder of this chapter, draws from Cornwall, *Century of Singing*; Michael Hicks, *The Mormon Tabernacle Choir: A Biography* (Urbana: University of Illinois Press, 2015); Charles Jeffrey Calman, *The Mormon Tabernacle Choir* (New York: Harper and Row, 1979); and esp., Millicent D. Cornwall, comp., "Chronological History of Salt Lake Tabernacle Choir, 1847–1957," CR 352-38, CHL. From the Church History Library, I also consulted "Mormon Tabernacle Choir tour files, 1896–1978," CR 352-1; "Mormon Tabernacle Choir history, 1936–1999," CR 352-11; "Salt Lake Tabernacle Choir publicity file, 1911–1967," CR 352-19; "Salt Lake Tabernacle Choir fan mail, 1939–1999," CR 352-59.

16   "The Chord of a Choir," *Life*, July 26, 1954, 20.

17   Broadcast #1,300, July 18, 1954 ("And now another generation is listening").

18   See Hicks, *Mormon Tabernacle Choir*, 104–105; David O. McKay Diaries, December 1, 1952, collected under "Tabernacle Choir" heading at https://mormonstudies.as.virginia .edu/david-o-mckay-diary-excerpts.

19   *Century of Singing*, 234, 49. For context, see Lloyd D. Newell, "From the Crossroads of the West: Eight Decades of Music and the Spoken Word," in *Salt Lake City: The Place Which God Prepared*, ed. Scott C. Esplin and Kenneth L. Alford (Salt Lake City: Deseret Book, 2011), 304–322.

20   See *Diaries of J. Reuben Clark*, 181–184; Feller, *Eternity in the Ether*, 69–79.

21   "Pres. McKay Spurs Missionary Drive," *Salt Lake Tribune*, April 6, 1954. For context, see Gregory Prince and William Robert Wright, *David O. McKay and the Rise of Modern Mormonism* (Salt Lake City: University of Utah Press, 2005); Taunalyn Rutherford, "'Her Borders Must Be Enlarged': Evolving Conceptions of Zion," in *Foundations of the Restoration: The 45th Annual Brigham Young University Sidney B. Sperry Symposium*, ed. Craig James Ostler, Michael Hubbard MacKay, and Barbara Morgan Gardner (Salt Lake City: Deseret Book, 2016), 139–156.

22   J. Russell Scott interview, 54. Fred Waring's Glee Club (later known as Fred Waring and His Pennsylvanians), a small choir that resembled the Tabernacle Choir in style and repertoire, had previously recorded the "Battle Hymn of the Republic" on an early LP from 1949.

23   "Woman's Word and Work—Boston" *Unitarian* 5.5 (May 1890): 253–254.

24   I watched the film on Amazon.com. For context, see Rebecca Prime, "Through America's Eyes: Cinerama and the Cold War," in *Cinema's Military Industrial Complex*, ed. Haidee Wasson and Lee Grieveson (Oakland: University of California Press, 2018), 61–74.

25   I found the TV coverage on YouTube: https://www.youtube.com/watch?v=-JTjB35zUxU. The broadcast date was July 23, 1962.

26   *Diary of Lela W. Clark*, 247.

27   Details from "Mormon Tabernacle Choir Tour Files," box 7, fd. 1.

28   Spencer W. Kimball, untitled speech, October 6, 1962, in *One Hundred Thirty-second Semi-annual Conference* (Salt Lake City: LDS Church, 1962), 55–56.

29 On the changing image of Mormonism, see Chiung Hwang Chen and Ethan Yorgason,
    "'Those Amazing Mormons': The Media's Construction of Latter-day Saints as a Model
    Minority," *Dialogue* 32.2 (Summer 1999): 107–128; Jan Shipps, *Sojourner in the Promised
    Land: Forty Years among the Mormons* (Urbana: University of Illinois Press, 2000),
    45–123; Jared Farmer, *Mormons in the Media, 1830–2012* (self-published e-book, 2012),
    available at jaredfarmer.net/digital-projects; J. B. Haws, *The Mormon Image in the
    American Mind: Fifty Years of Public Perception* (New York: Oxford University Press,
    2013).
30 See Layne Karafantis, "Telstar, the Cold War, and the Origins of Global
    Communications," *Vulcan* 4.1 (August 2016): 112–134.

7

CORRELATION OF REVERENCE

When Tracy Y. Cannon, the genteel face of the Church Music Committee, died in 1961, he received the equivalent of a state funeral in the Tabernacle. It was a testament to his organizational skills that he had exerted such influence without being a General Authority—though this was not unprecedented, as evidenced by Susa Young Gates, a towering figure in Mormon letters.[1]

In Cannon's lifetime, members of the upper hierarchy had not always agreed with his master class and masterworks emphasis. J. Reuben Clark played opera at home on LPs, but otherwise he had little taste for musicians, much less concerts. Like David O. McKay, he disliked the music of Bach, and in church settings he preferred silence to organ.[2] In 1946, the First Presidency—which included Clark and McKay—issued a directive that forbade music during the passing of the sacrament. Prior to this, the ward organist would typically play soft selections, including Bach. Clark believed that music distracted the mind from the ordinance and provided cover for inappropriate whispering. "Pure religion" required "perfect order" required "reverence," which could best be enforced in "absolute quiet" and "perfect silence."[3] Over time, Latter-day Saints accepted the social construction that to revere was to sit still. McKay conveyed a maxim: "The greatest manifestation of spirituality is reverence. Indeed, reverence is spirituality." At one of the many General Conferences McKay couldn't attend due to the infirmities of old age, he authorized one of his sons to speak for him. Robert R. McKay described, in the first-person voice, the prophet's best-ever sacrament: a gathering of 800 people at which "not a sound could be heard except the ticking of the clock."[4]

Perhaps the only time General Conference achieved McKay's goal of perfect order was on the evening of April 7, 1962, immediately prior to the

https://doi.org/10.5876/781646427031.c007

General Priesthood Meeting—children not invited—when Vern Knudsen performed acoustical tests. One of the General Authorities read a script that explained the basics of reverberation and absorption, and then he told the audience of men and teenage boys that "complete silence" was necessary to measure the decay of organ tones. The listeners had to be "perfectly motionless and almost breathless." After analyzing the results, the Tabernacle's building managers reported their recommendations to the Brethren. The report listed *Music and the Spoken Word* as having primary acoustical importance, ahead of General Conference. To eliminate the disturbing "flutter echoes" from the temple of LDS broadcasting, managers recommended subtle changes to the shape and composition of the domed ceiling, and the removal of certain areas of carpet.[5]

Silence, an awkward ideal for a natalist organization, required other architectural interventions. In the 1950s, the "cry room"—a separate space with a PA system where nursing children and noisy toddlers could retreat with their mothers during sacrament meeting—became a standard feature of LDS chapels. This was a religious borrowing from the movie palace, which since the mid-1920s had accommodated nursing mothers in an amplified room with a soundproof window overlooking the screen. In 1951, the Salt Lake Tabernacle got its own window-box cry room—an innovation that would have pleased Brigham Young, who loved children (including the fifty-six he sired) but resented their commotion during his prophetic speaking. Even as radio technicians removed dampening fabrics from the Tabernacle, Church architects—following the First Presidency's directive for quietude—added heavy drapery, synthetic carpet, and acoustic tiling to chapels. As a result of these sound-deadening additions, ward pipe organs sounded little better than electronic instruments.

Alexander Schreiner, the famous lead organist at the Salt Lake Tabernacle, was the voice of pragmatism on the Church Music Committee following Cannon's death; the new chair, Leroy Robertson—the most respected LDS composer, recently retired as head of the music department at the University of Utah—was the voice of idealism. Schreiner had persistent doubts about the musical capacity of wards beyond the Salt Lake–Provo axis. He suspected that Cannon's efforts had been window dressing, or activity for activity's sake. The organist believed the gospel was for uncultured people, too, and considered it "somewhat sinful" to judge anyone on their music preferences.[6] Robertson, for his part, tried to hold the line, sharing his predecessor's belief that the "established masterpieces" of European classical music were "sacred."[7] The composer wanted to direct the singing Saints toward excellence—exemplified by the oratorio, a genre that aligned with the LDS theology of vocality—and away from the musical fare heard at the annual temple pageants and Pioneer Day pageants, which he derided as "Mormon rodeo."[8]

Robertson was thinking of events like the 1947 centennial pageant *Guachama* at San Bernardino's Covered Wagon Days, featuring the Tabernacle Choir plus "whooping Indians, burning buildings, [and] a pioneer train wending its way into the canyon," narrated by Richard Evans.[9] Another example was *Mindful of His Own*, the Days of '47 pageant held in the Tabernacle in 1959, with the choir providing background music, with KSL newscaster Rex Campbell as the "Voice of God," and a cast of hundreds—including white suburban Mormons dressed up as "Indians on the warpath," attacking an emigrant train. The list of racist *and* cheesy Mormon musical productions could be amply extended.[10]

Robertson had at least one high-ranking ally: apostle Spencer W. Kimball. In a 1967 speech at Brigham Young University—whose Department of Music had succeeded the McCune School of Music as the exemplar of LDS musicality—Kimball issued a series of rhetorical statements that were touching in their idealism. Why can't a Mormon write a greater oratorio than *Messiah*? There must be many Wagners in our midst, if we can cultivate them. Surely there's another Verdi out there. Could we not find and develop a Bach? Why cannot we discover, train, and present many Paganinis? Surely not all the Paderewskis were born in Poland in the last century.[11] The "Kimball challenge" inspired many LDS artists, educators, and philanthropists, who responded with endeavors like the Mormon Festival of Arts, the Ricks College Sacred Music Series, the Barlow Endowment for Music Composition, and later the Mormon Arts Center.[12]

But other apostles, more numerous and more powerful, had a different agenda. Mark E. Petersen, Boyd K. Packer, and Ezra Taft Benson—anti-intellectual and ultraconservative to the core—led an effort to command and control all music in the Church. Robertson, an academic, was out of his depth and swimming against the bureaucratic tide. The Church let him go in 1969 and replaced him with Petersen, who proceeded to shut down the committee. In reaction, Robertson expressed bitterness: "I fear . . . things will revert back, as the Book of Mormon states, to where 'The sow goes to her mire and the dog to its vomit.'"[13]

Music was one field in a much larger battle, decades long, over bureaucratization and retrenchment. In the postwar period, Progressive-Era General Authorities with scientific and scholarly pedigrees were replaced with "Clark men" who streamlined correlation into "Priesthood Correlation." They wanted to reform the auxiliaries, which they believed had achieved too much autonomy. "You've just got to cut the tail off of this dog," said one.[14] The auxiliary model of organization, with all its redundancy, relied on the social skills of volunteer women. Under the new system, rolled out in the late 1960s, the Relief Society lost its budget, its magazine, its festivals, its Singing Mothers. The Church Office Building, Utah's first skyscraper built from 1962 to 1972, loomed directly above the Relief Society Building. The organizational flowchart for the new office workers—and everyone else in the Church—was called the "Priesthood Correlation Line of Control and Authority." Like a good corporation, the LDS Church hired a consultancy to evaluate the efficiency of this arrangement.[15]

The consequences for music appeared clearly in the *Handbook of Instructions*—the how-to manual on running a ward for lay leaders. In 1960, the handbook had included this correlation directive in Tracy Cannon's voice: "Music is a most important part of our religious services and our recreational activities. The highest standards in music literature and musical performance must be maintained." For the 1970 edition, the group voice of Priesthood Correlation issued revised guidance: "Music is an important part of our Church services. The music presented should always be in harmony with the teachings of the Church and appropriate to the occasion."[16]

A revamped Church Music Department came into being in fall 1972, with Leslie Stone, a General Authority with no background in music, appointed as managing director. Whereas Cannon had invoked "correlation" to prioritize a uniformly high level of training, literacy, repertoire, and performance, Stone used Priesthood Correlation to prioritize centralized supervision over the propriety of music. The Church eliminated Ward Music Committees—erstwhile "Guilds"—and replaced them with a singular music "chairman" (often a woman) who reported to a stake music chairman (more likely a man), and so on, upward to the First Presidency. Accompanying these bureaucratic changes, the Church stopped installing pipe organs in chapels, for the department determined that cheaper electronic organs were sufficient for "accompaniment." This controversial policy—the end of a cost-benefit analysis going back to the 1940s—was misconstrued by old-time supporters of Cannon and Robertson as a "ban" on pipe organs.[17]

By the 1970s, the remarkable international growth of the Church through conversions demanded a comprehensive rethink of music. A religion expanding into developing countries could not, explained Elder Stone, afford the luxury of musicianship. Writing for the *Ensign* (the newly consolidated and correlated Church magazine for adult members), he was matter of fact: "Sacred music is a tool." The Brethren wanted "functional music"; the function was inspiration. Rather than engaging in music for music's sake, members should focus on a smaller repertoire of "hymns of the Restoration."[18] The term *functional music* shared a genealogy with "industrial music" (e.g., the BBC's "Music While You Work") and "programmed music" (e.g., Muzak), both of which were widely used in US and UK wartime defense plants and postwar factories to maximize productivity.[19] Meanwhile, mid-century music educators and music therapists used the term *functional music* to mean the equivalent of *Gebrauchsmusik*, or utilitarian music for students or patients. LDS usage combined both of these meanings: easy-to-perform music that maximized the production of reverence. The Church Music Department greenlighted a simplified hymnbook so that senior missionaries with Casio synthesizers could teach converts in the "Third World" the rudiments of congregational hymn singing. In a pinch, converts could simply sing in unison along to Church-issued cassette tapes. Two separate problems for an internationalizing organization—explicitly Americanist lyric content and implicitly Anglo-Protestant music content—were unexamined and thus deferred.

The Church is a large ship, and it took a few years for reactionaries to functionalize choral music in the Tabernacle. The takeover was marked, symbolically, by the passings of Jessie Evans Smith and her husband, President Joseph Fielding Smith (the successor to David O. McKay), in 1971 and 1972, respectively. Sister Smith, with a background in comic opera, had been a loyal lifetime member of the choir. She and her husband made certain that she appeared regularly in the Tabernacle from the late 1930s through April 1970, peppily singing with vibrato her favorite light classical sacred song, "King of Glory."[20] Representing the other side of the repertoire, "Inflammatus et accensus" from Rossini's *Stabat Mater*, for soprano soloist with chorus, was performed twenty-six times in General Conference from 1907 to 1972.[21] From 1973 onward, any type of solo performance became exceedingly rare. Organ was now the only allowed instrument—and only in an accompanying role. The Brethren directed the choir to sing doctrinally correct hymns in General Conference; those hymns were topically and theologically tied to committee-approved talks as "unit packages." This was a belated realization of Heber J. Grant's 1912 appeal to choirs "never to sing the words of a song, no matter how beautiful and inspiring the music may be, where the teachings are not in perfect accord with the truths of the gospel."[22] Thus, music's secondary authority derived from the primacy of priesthood vocality. General Conference became, effectively, "The Spoken Word, and Music."

In 1976, Boyd K. Packer gave a talk that served as a victory statement as well as a rebuttal to Spencer W. Kimball and other apostles going back one century who had predicted that the Restoration would engender Shakespeares and Miltons as well as Wagners and Verdis. We don't need gifted musicians to make functional music, said Packer. Our gifted members are temperamental. They stray. The art of the Restoration will be produced by the inspired, not by the gifted. Where Cannon had been utopian, Packer was realistic. He didn't care whether home composers could or would write oratorios to rival the masters. He wanted quiet hymns of devotion, all the time. One of the signs of today's apostasy is the willingness of other Christian faiths to compromise on rock music, he said.[23]

Quietude was the zone of aurality where Packer and Kimball came together. After the latter became president of the Church in 1973, he made reverence a policy of his prophetic administration, with the goal of Mormons becoming the happiest *and* the most reverent people in all the earth—explicitly connecting those two states of being.[24] He always spoke in a hushed, wavering voice because he had lost three-quarters of his vocal cords to throat cancer in the 1950s. A miniature microphone attached to his eyeglasses aided amplification. Whereas Brigham Young had not expected children to listen to priesthood authorities and simply wanted mothers to take their noisy presence away, Kimball admonished parents to train their children to listen quietly to speakers. LDS parents did not always succeed, of course, and the sounds of their silencing efforts became a characteristic feature of sacrament meeting. Having already banned organ from the passing of the bread and water, the Brethren next went after the prelude music. Elder Packer was known to publicly upbraid ward organists for playing Bach with intensity, something he found irreverent; other General Authorities of the time were known to tell stake presidents to forbid Mozart and Bach at any volume.[25] At the local level, many bishops started enforcing a "hymn-only" rule for preludes and postludes.

When the Church Office Building opened in 1975, it was quiet but not silent: Muzak played softly over the intercom system in all public and common spaces, twenty-four hours a day, up to 500 songs per day. The owner of the Muzak franchise for the State of Utah was Stanley Rees, former sound engineer for the Salt Lake Tabernacle and a friend and business associate of Richard L. Evans and Gordon B. Hinckley. Following the US corporate playbook of the time, the First Presidency approved the Muzak license, albeit for the package with the "most conservative selections." Even so, someone in the building immediately complained to the Brethren about the propriety of some of the instrumentalized pop songs, for they still heard the lyrics in their mind.[26]

The listening preferences of teenagers—or their parents, for that matter—did not figure into General Conference, where the Brethren enjoyed total sonic control: eight or more hours of elderly men intoning like Evans, with hymns as breaks. There was no LDS equivalent of youth Mass with guitars, a Catholic accommodation after Vatican II. In 1970, Ezra Taft Benson, using racist code language, told young people to avoid "the jungle rhythm which inflames the savagery within" and then, for added effect, quoted the late J. Reuben Clark's characterization of 1950s popular music as not too far above the "tom-tom of the jungle."[27] The following year, in General Conference, Benson memorably denounced rock music as "the devil's thrust."[28] His own radio listening preferences centered on symphonic masters of the Romantic era: Beethoven, Brahms, Dvořák, Tchaikovsky, Sibelius, Rachmaninoff—the kind of music programmed on KBYU-FM.[29] As the perceived crisis of sex, drugs, and rock intensified in 1973, President Harold B. Lee told a youth gathering, "We plead with you to listen to good music," by which he meant great classical works by the masters, not sensuous music prostituted to Satan's purposes that aroused the wrong passions. Invoking the primacy of priesthood vocality, he instructed, "I have the responsibility to speak by the Spirit of the Lord, and you have the responsibility to listen by the Spirit of the Lord."[30]

Some LDS teens became minor rebels. TV heartthrob Donny Osmond cheerfully sang "I'm a little bit rock 'n' roll"—the "little" marking his Mormon circumspection.[31] The Osmond family had five straight Gold-certified LPs, capped by *The Plan* (1973), a concept album about the "Plan of Salvation," the core of post-Manifesto LDS theology. This album signaled that Mormon youth of the 1970s wanted more emotional, more personal connections to Jesus through music. In the evangelical world, born-again teens could attend revival festivals in packed stadiums featuring electric guitars and drums, and speaking and singing in tongues.[32] But the experience of becoming a Jesus freak was unavailable to Latter-day Saints. Thirty-something Mormons produced homemade musicals—notably *Saturday's Warrior* (1973), the LDS soft-rock answer to *Jesus Christ Superstar*—in an attempt to offer semi-ecstatic sounds to youth without compromising standards.[33]

The Brethren carved out an exception for the Osmonds, but they remained firm about the evils of hippie beards, long hair, short skirts, and hard rock—and the virtues of hymns. Elder Packer gave LDS youth his advice on how to control their thoughts in a world full of sinful input. He compared their minds to media players:

> Choose from among the sacred music of the Church a favorite hymn, one with words that are uplifting and music that is reverent, one that makes you feel something akin to inspiration . . . Go over it in your mind carefully. Memorize it. Even though you have had no musical

training, you can think through a hymn. Now, use this hymn as the place for your thoughts to go. Make it your emergency channel. Whenever you find these shady actors have slipped from the sidelines of your thinking onto the stage of your mind, put on this record, as it were.[34]

This apostle of reverence gave new meaning to old words: *There shall be a record kept among you.*

NOTES

1   See Romney Burke, *Susa Young Gates: Daughter of Mormonism* (Salt Lake City: Signature Books, 2022).

2   D. Michael Quinn, *J. Reuben Clark: The Church Years* (Provo: Brigham Young University Press, 1983), 244–250.

3   First Presidency to Presidents of Stakes and Bishops of Wards, May 2, 1946, in James R. Clark, comp., *Messages of the First Presidency*, vol. 6 (Salt Lake City: Bookcraft, 1975), 252–253.

4   David O. McKay, untitled talk, April 8, 1967, in *One Hundred Thirty-seventh Annual Conference* (Salt Lake City: The Church of Jesus Christ of Latter-day Saints, 1967), 84–88, quotes on 86. A version of this talk had previously appeared in the LDS children's magazine *The Instructor*.

5   "Correspondence and reports, 1940–1962," William L. Woolf Salt Lake Tabernacle Papers, MS 30813, Church History Library (CHL).

6   Alexander Schreiner, interviewed by Nancy Furner Fenn, June 1973–May 1975, OH 293, 25, CHL.

7   Quoted in Marian Robertson Wilson, *Leroy Robertson, Music Giant from the Rockies* (Salt Lake City: Blue Ribbon Publications, 1996), 281.

8   Lowell M. Durham, interviewed by Michael M. Moody, November–December 1977, OH 408, 28, CHL. Arguably, the most distinctive feature of LDS composition is not musicological but generic: the employment of outmoded genres—oratorios and cantatas—that feature sacred vocality. Composers who wrote one or more such works include Evan Stephens, B. Cecil Gates, Crawford Gates, W. King Driggs, Leroy Robertson, A. Laurence Lyon, Darwin Wolford, Merrill Jensen, Merrill Bradshaw, Robert Cundick, and Brett Stewart. This genre preference accords with a larger point that Mormonism selects for old media, starting with seer stones.

9   Cornwall, "Chronological History of Salt Lake Tabernacle Choir," 249.

10 The Hill Cumorah Pageant (1937–2019) in Palmyra, New York, and the Mormon Miracle Pageant (1967–2019) in Manti, Utah, are particularly noteworthy. See Megan Sanborn Jones, *Contemporary Mormon Pageantry: Seeking after the Dead* (Ann Arbor: University of Michigan Press, 2018).

11 Paraphrased from Spencer W. Kimball, "Education for Eternity" (BYU devotional address), September 12, 1967, reprinted in John W. Welch and Don E. Norton, eds., *Educating Zion* (Provo: Brigham Young University Studies, 1996), 43–63; also available at https://speeches.byu.edu. An excerpted, adapted version appeared as Spencer W.

Kimball, "First Presidency Message: The Gospel Vision of the Arts," *Ensign* 7.7 (July 1977): 2–5.

12   See Glen Nelson, "Mormon Artists Group: Adventures in Art Making," *Dialogue* 39.3 (Fall 2006): 115–128; Terryl Givens, Paul Anderson, and Richard Bushman, eds., *The Kimball Challenge at Fifty: Mormon Arts Center Essays* (New York: Mormon Arts Center, 2017).

13   Wilson, *Leroy Robertson*, 290.

14   Lowell M. Durham interview, 27, recollecting the words of Joseph B. Wirthlin.

15   For context, see Armand L. Mauss, *The Angel and the Beehive: The Mormon Struggle with Assimilation* (Urbana: University of Illinois Press, 1994); D. Michael Quinn, *The Mormon Hierarchy: Extensions of Power* (Salt Lake City: Signature Books, 1997); Tina Hatch, "'Changing Times Bring Changing Conditions': Relief Society, 1960 to the Present," *Dialogue* 37.3 (Fall 2004): 65–98; Michael A. Goodman, "Correlation: The Turning Point (1960s)," in Esplin and Alford, *The Place Which God Prepared*, 259–284.

16   *General Handbook of Instructions* 18 (1960), 25; *General Handbook of Instructions* 21 (1970), 99. The entire collection of handbooks (M250 G362d) is available online through the CHL.

17   See "The Organ and Mormon Church Music," *Dialogue* 10.1 (Spring 1975): 34–39, part of a special issue on "Music and Worship in the Restored Church."

18   "Music in the Church: A Conversation with Elder O. Leslie Stone," *Ensign* 3.8 (August 1973): 74–75.

19   See Doron K. Antrim, "Music in Industry," *Musical Quarterly* 29.3 (July 1943): 275–290; E. Thayer Gaston, "Functional Music," *Teachers College Record* 59.9 (1958): 292–309; Simon C. Jones and Thomas G. Schumacher, "Muzak: On Functional Music and Power," *Critical Studies in Media Communication* 9.2 (1992): 156–169; Keith Jones, "Music in Factories: A Twentieth-Century Technique for Control of the Productive Self," *Social and Cultural Geography* 6.5 (October 2005): 723–744.

20   For context, see Linda W. Harris, "The Legend of Jessie Evans Smith," *Utah Historical Quarterly* 44.4 (Fall 1976): 351–364. "King of Glory" was written by Nebraska-based sheet-music composer James Asher Parks.

21   General Conference music data set, CHL, shared with me by courtesy; in time, this spreadsheet will be available to the public at the Church History Biographical Database: https://history.churchofjesuschrist.org/chd.

22   Heber J. Grant, "Sing Only What We Believe," *Improvement Era* 15.9 (July 1912): 784–787, quote on 786.

23   Paraphrased from Boyd K. Packer, "The Arts and the Spirit of the Lord" (twelve-stake fireside address), February 1, 1976, reprinted in *BYU Studies* 16.4 (Summer 1976): 575–588; also available at https://speeches.byu.edu.

24   Spencer W. Kimball, *We Should Be a Reverent People* (Salt Lake City: The Church of Jesus Christ of Latter-day Saints, 1976), copy in CHL.

25   See Merrill J. Bateman, "The Power of Hymns" (Church Music Workshop talk), August 4, 1998, reprinted in *Ensign* 31.7 (July 2001): 14–20; Memorandum from Billings Stake Music Chairman to Ezra Taft Benson, October 1973, "Music Department correspondence, 1967, 1970–1977," CR 108-1, box 1, fd. 13, CHL.

26   O. Leslie Stone to Mark E. Petersen and Thomas S. Monson, March 5, 1975, CR 108-1, box 1, fd. 2, CHL.

27 Ezra Taft Benson, untitled talk, October 2, 1970, *One Hundred Fortieth Semi-annual Conference* (Salt Lake City: LDS Church, 1970), 21–26, quote on 24.

28 Ezra Taft Benson, "Satan's Thrust—Youth" (General Conference talk), *Ensign* 1.12 (December 1971): 53–56, quote on 53.

29 "Secretary's Favorite Music, Played on the Radio," January 2, 1955, Ezra Taft Benson Papers, Dwight D. Eisenhower Presidential Library, Abilene, KS, copy shared with me by Patrick Mason.

30 " 'Listen By Spirit,' Pres. Lee Tells Youth," *Church News*, June 16, 1973.

31 "A Little Bit Country, a Little Bit Rock 'n' Roll" appeared on the LP *Donny & Marie Featuring Songs from Their Television Show* (Polydor, 1976).

32 See Heather Hendershot, *Shaking the World for Jesus: Media and Conservative Evangelical Culture* (Chicago: University of Chicago Press, 2004), 52–84; David W. Stowe, *No Sympathy for the Devil: Christian Pop Music and the Transformation of American Evangelicalism* (Chapel Hill: University of North Carolina Press, 2011); Randall J. Stephens, *The Devil's Music: How Christians Inspired, Condemned, and Embraced Rock 'n' Roll* (Cambridge, MA: Harvard University Press, 2018); Leah Payne, *God Gave Rock and Roll to You: A History of Contemporary Christian Music* (New York: Oxford University Press, 2024).

33 *Saturday's Warrior* had lyrics by Doug Stewart and music by Lex de Azevedo. See Callie Oppedisano, " 'Worthy of Imitation': Contemporary Mormon Drama on the Latter Day Stage" (PhD dissertation, Tufts University, New Orleans, LA, 2009); Givens, *People of Paradox*, 268–271; Johnson, *Mormons, Musical Theater, and Belonging in America*, 113–141.

34 Boyd K. Packer, "Inspiring Music—Worthy Thoughts" (General Conference talk), October 5, 1973, *Ensign* 3.4 (January 1974): 25–29. For context, see Rebecca de Schweinitz, "Holding on to the 'Chosen Generation': The Mormon Battle for Youth in the Late 1960s and Early 1970s," in *Out of Obscurity: Mormonism since 1945*, ed. Patrick Q. Mason and John G. Turner (New York: Oxford University Press, 2016), 278–301.

8

RELIGIOUS RACE MUSIC

Paradoxically, even as the Tabernacle Choir became more hymn-centric for internal audiences, it became more secular and less classical on CBS radio and Columbia LPs. As of 1977, the year Alexander Schreiner retired, more than 1,000 radio and TV stations carried the Sunday morning program from the Tabernacle.[1] Priesthood correlation of music existed in tension with the Church's dual mandate to the choir to garner publicity and generate royalties to cover operating costs, both of which required accommodation with commercial markets. When Eugene Ormandy moved to a different label in 1968, the choir lost its connection to classical music consumers. Columbia had to be mindful of the competition: the Robert Shaw Chorale on RCA Victor (mainly classical) and the Roger Wagner Chorale on Capitol (half classical, half folk). The commercial lane available to the Mormon Tabernacle Choir was semiclassical white Americana: Broadway tunes, Hollywood themes, Disney ballads, collegiate fight songs, and medleys of crooner ballads the likes of which the Church had once decried as trashy.[2]

Evans, always protective of the choir's reputation, might have objected to this turn, but he died prematurely in 1971, literally from overwork. His final death throes in the hospital were precipitated by distress, manifest in checking his ticking wristwatch every few seconds, that he was late for airtime. "The voice has been stilled by death," eulogized the *Deseret News*, "but the message of 'The Spoken Word' from Temple Square lives and will continue to inspire mankind."[3]

With Richard Condie now in control of the Sunday broadcast, the choir enjoyed much more prominence than did the organ or the substitute word. This was the iteration of LDS music consumed by osmosis by Trey Parker (b. 1969) and Matt Stone (b. 1971), non-Mormon comedians from

Colorado. When staging *The Book of Mormon* (2011) on Broadway, Parker and Stone told their producers:

> "No, make it more Rodgers and Hammerstein." Or, "Make it more Disney." Or, "Make it more Mormon." And they're like: "Well, which one is it?" And we're like, "No, it's all the same word for the same thing." You know, basically like make this brighter and happier and cheesier.[4]

Another adjective was so strongly implicit here it was practically explicit: *whiter*.

In its first 100 years as an all-white organization, the Mormon Tabernacle Choir had been heard much more than seen. Thus, its distinguishing whiteness was, in the radio era, a matter of repertoire and especially timbre, also known as "tone quality" or "tone color" (*Klangfarbe*). In US radio history, the color line strongly affected the bodily production and psychoacoustic reception of tone coloring.[5] CBS trained its listeners to hear the difference between "Mormon" and "Negro" religious sounds and to recognize the Tabernacle as a transmitter of acousmatic whiteness.[6] About ten years into the run of *Music and the Spoken Word*, the network added to its Sunday sustaining lineup a contrasting program that served to accentuate the racial normativity of Latter-day Saints. *Wings over Jordan* (1938–1947) was the first national radio program produced and hosted by Black voice talent—not blackface voice actors like those on *Amos 'n' Andy*.

Programmatically, the two Sunday broadcasts, which aired two hours apart, could have been twins, but sonically and racially they were non-kin. The Wings over Jordan Choir was small in number and powerful in sound (not oversized yet restrained); it exclusively sang a cappella (never accompanied by organ); it was allowed to perform only Black spirituals (instead of being encouraged to sing a variety of things, including Stephen Foster minstrel staples); its venue varied nearly every week, as the Cleveland-based choir hit the road (instead of having an iconic home-recording location); its commenter, Rev. Glenn T. Settle, spoke in directly religious terms without being denominational (unlike Evans, who was implicitly sectarian yet more inspirational than pastoral); and its program included a slot for a guest speech by an African American intellectual (instead of yet another sermonette by the same commenter). Through these two enormously popular shows—each with audiences in the millions—US listeners of the World War II era were taught to hear that both Blacks and Mormons were honest Americans, that Mormons sounded anything but Black, that Blackness was essentially Christian, and that Mormonism was practically Protestant. In its differing treatments of these two outsider groups, CBS bolstered the New Deal brand of tolerance through segregation. Tellingly, the network never invited Reverend Settle—or any other Black religious leader—to appear on *Church of the Air* while reserving a seat in the radio booth for Latter-day Saints, who used the opportunity every year to emphasize their western narrative, using familiar racial code language: "Pioneers of Freedom," "Building the Western Empire," "Religion in the Conquest of Our West," and on and on.[7]

For occasional southern color, the western choir sang spirituals in rotation, the top five being "Gabriel's Trumpet," "Listen to the Lambs," "My Lord, What a Mornin'," "Poor Wayfaring Stranger," and "Were You There?"[8] Subsequently, in the LP era, the choir recorded "Sometimes I Feel Like a Motherless Child" (plus some Foster songs) for a Civil War centennial album.[9] Cornwall, despite being a former minstrel leader, interpreted these selections with the choir's typical "un-colored" tone quality. The inclusion of Black spirituals in the repertoire said more about CBS's priorities than the Church's, for LDS members were forbidden, by the handbook, to sing such songs in sacrament meeting.[10]

Marian Anderson, the celebrated contralto and civil rights activist from Philadelphia, had performed spirituals in Salt Lake City at least six times. "Where is the Tabernacle?" she asked in 1937, upon arrival at the train station. Her accompanist added, "We have heard so much about it, that we want to learn all about it and hear the organ."[11] But Anderson had not been invited to sing inside the famous auditorium—her venue was Kingsbury Hall at the University of Utah—and was not allowed to stay in any hotel in the capital city due to Mormon Utah's Jim Crow customs. On return visits to Kingsbury Hall in 1939, 1943, and 1944—the latter two during a US war against fascism and racism—LDS leaders evidently gave Anderson permission to stay in the Church-owned Hotel Utah on the condition that she use the freight lift.[12] Her local experience with discrimination was hardly unique. When Roy Wilkins, editor of *The Crisis* (and future executive secretary of the NAACP), took a western road trip in 1939, he and his wife looked forward to seeing the City of the Saints, having been loyal radio listeners of *Music and the Spoken Word.* They were shocked to find out that no one in downtown Salt Lake would serve them: This was the place from which the "celestial voices of four hundred well-tuned Mormons rolled out across the airwaves every week—and we couldn't get a cup of coffee because we were black." After that bitter wake-up, Wilkins stopped listening to the choir.[13] As for the famed Marian Anderson, only on her fifth visit to Salt Lake, in 1948, did she secure an invitation to sing in the Tabernacle and permission to walk through the front doors of the Hotel Utah to the main elevator to get to her room, which overlooked the temple.[14] Her concert at Temple Square included opera arias and songs by English composers as well as spirituals.

In General Conference, the Mormon Tabernacle Choir performed a Black spiritual exactly once, in October 1967, after a summer of urban uprisings across the United States. Apocalyptic rumors based on apocryphal prophecies about Black militants intent on desecrating the Salt Lake Temple had flared up among Utah Saints like a latent virus; in response, the Brethren stationed snipers on the rooftops of buildings around the Tabernacle.[15] In the first session of the first day (Friday), Ezra Taft Benson gave a blistering John Bircher speech that called the civil rights movement a "Communist conspiracy" and a "satanical threat."[16] Two mornings later, incongruously, the choir sang "Deep River," whose emancipatory lyrics, when mouthed by Mormons, were perhaps construed by some listeners as a pioneer anthem about the Camp of Israel westering to the promised land of Salt Lake Valley, with its Jordan River feeding its dead sea:

> Deep river, my home is over Jordan.
> Deep river, Lord, I want to cross over into campground.
> Oh, don't you want to go to that gospel feast,
> That promised land where all is peace?

The Church Music Committee immediately received a flurry of letters from members, asking: Has the policy changed? May we now sing spirituals in church? The answer was unequivocal: no.[17]

A month after "Deep River," a brave Black woman auditioned to join the choir. Although she passed the singing test, Condie knew he needed top-level permission to desegregate the Church's most famous sub-organization at a time when the Brethern still barred Black men from being ordained to the lay priesthood and refused the right of temple worship to all Black people. The priesthood and temple bans dated to Brigham Young and were not based on revelation and therefore could have been revoked by a policy statement. But in 1949, the First Presidency, in the authorial voice of J. Reuben Clark, had elevated this racist practice to racist doctrine, which in turn encouraged elaboration of racist theology about the "one-drop" curse of Cain and the prehistory of Black inferiority in the preexistence. The codification of anti-Blackness almost immediately ran up against the civil rights movement, not to mention the Church's own ambitions to proselytize in Brazil and Africa. In the face of Christian contradiction, some apostles chose to deflect, obfuscate, equivocate, dissemble, or lie—while others expressed unapologetic certitude. Regarding the singer who auditioned, the Brethren quietly instructed Condie to tell her, disingenuously, that the choir was not currently accepting applications.[18]

In late 1968, the paranoically anti-Black Benson invited arch-segregationist George Wallace, former (and future) governor of Alabama then running for US president, to give a campaign speech in the Tabernacle. (Benson, a former cabinet secretary under Eisenhower, had wanted and expected to be Wallace's running mate until McKay squashed the idea.) As a standard courtesy to political dignitaries, the choir sang patriotic songs. Cries of "Wallace for America" echoed under the dome, while student protesters from the University of Utah picketed outside. After Richard Nixon, a bigot more adept at dog whistling, won the White House, the choir excitedly accepted an invitation to perform at its second inaugural in a row—not anticipating that it would henceforth only be invited by right-wing presidents. In an astonishingly short period of time, from the summer of Telstar to the election of 1968, the choir went from being a consensus symbol of Americanism to a contested symbol of white religious nationalism.[19]

Hoping to repair the Church's well-earned reputation as racially prejudiced—which made Latter-day Saints the uncomfortable bedmates of Southern Baptists and Afrikaners—the First Presidency permitted the choir to admit its first-ever Black member, Marilyn Yuille, in January 1970, just in time to perform at the funeral of McKay. Yuille was soon joined by Wynetta Willis Martin, who later wrote a memoir. Martin had listened to *Music and the Spoken Word* as a child in Los Angeles and dreamed of singing in the Tabernacle. Before finding the LDS Church, she had tried many denominations but joined none of them. To comfort herself in her period of seeking, she would sing "Sometimes I Feel Like a Motherless Child." Her discovery of Mormonism was preceded by an agonizing night of prayer in which she was stalked by a "horrid massive presence of a silent suffocating stillness" that ceased with a voice—quiet and serene yet majestic—speaking directly to her in the darkness: "BE STILL, AND KNOW THAT I AM GOD." After this "revelation," she found the LDS Church, received the Holy Ghost, moved to Ogden, Utah, and joined the choir—her religious dreams come true, except for the presence of the priesthood in her home and the privilege of attending the temple. She longed for those blessings yet denied that the Church was prejudiced. Her LDS brothers and sisters repaid her faith by inviting her to scores of unpaid speaking and signing engagements. Her memoir ended: "I am so very glad that I AM A BLACK MORMON."[20]

Over the following months and years, anti-racist protestors—including many Black collegiate athletes—made "Bigot Young University" an anathema, while certain Latter-day Saints agitated from within the Church. For example, in early April 1976, Douglas A. Wallace of Vancouver, Washington, held a news conference at a motel, then immediately performed a priesthood ordination on a Black convert in the motel's swimming pool. Days later, Wallace crashed General Conference in Salt Lake City, rushing past the ushers, intending to have a podium confrontation with the prophet. "Make way for the Lord!" said Wallace, using "a loud voice," to quote the Church's subsequent legal complaint against him. Wallace was apprehended by security guards, barred by restraining order from attending General Conference again, and excommunicated for his offenses.[21]

In 1978, when ABC's Barbara Walters wanted to ask a question about the LDS Church's notorious priesthood ban, she did not approach President Spencer W. Kimball or J. Spencer Kinard, the former KSL reporter who served as Evans's replacement voice on *Music and the Spoken Word*. Rather, she traveled to the Osmond Entertainment Center in Orem, Utah, to speak to Donny and Marie, ages twenty and eighteen, respectively. The youngest Osmonds could say nothing except for gospel principles they had been taught: "We offer more, I think, than any another religion to the Black person" (Donny); "The woman is equally as important, but as far as speaking her mind, that should be the man's job" (Marie).[22] In other words, the Brethren speak for the Church, just as a husband speaks for his family.

Within months, the First Presidency announced a revelation that finally ended the priesthood and temple bans—the signal moment in the prophetic tenure of Spencer W. Kimball. The new truth was eventually canonized in the Doctrine and Covenants as "Official Declaration 2," following the Manifesto. In the time since Woodruff, the Brethren had turned revelation from a singular to a corporate act, requiring the unanimity of all fifteen revelators, which is partly why the inevitable reversal had stalled for such a disgracefully long time. Then, in an instant, all the hardline holdouts declared in one voice: the Lord had "heard their prayers" and revealed to them that "the long-promised day has come when every faithful, worthy man in the Church may receive the holy priesthood" and that all His children must "hearken to the voice of his authorized servants." Acting on his own, apostle Bruce R. McConkie, author of the influential *Mormon Doctrine* (1958/1966), which had included theological justifications for racism, started telling stories about how this come-to-Jesus moment in the Upper Room of the Salt Lake Temple in 1978 had been a Pentecost—just like Kirtland in 1836, complete with an angelic choir, a rushing wind, and an audible voice. These charismatic tall tales angered President Kimball, who insisted that the revelation-by-committee had been a quiet affair and that modern prophecy was a *feeling* from the Holy Ghost, not an auditory experience.[23]

Ironically, Kimball prolonged rather than ended a different form of nineteenth-century racialism: the prophecy, based on the Book of Mormon, that the Lamanites, as descendants of Israel, would "blossom as the rose" and, in the process, literally whiten. Kimball was the last high-ranking believer in this paternalistic theology of lineage and race. During his tenure in the First Presidency, the Church built up a large assimilationist infrastructure for the foster care and education of Native Americans, particularly Navajos (Diné). Brigham Young University (BYU), located in Provo, had more tribally enrolled students on scholarships than any other US university during the 1960s and 1970s. In Church-produced media from this period, Indigenous Latter-day Saints occupied an unstable triple identity as present-tense "Indians," past-tense "Lamanites," and future-tense "white and delightsome" people. The university, the publicity committee, and the seminary program helped with the production of pageants, musicals, plays, movies, and filmstrips featuring ancient Lamanite characters from the Book of Mormon, sometimes casting Native actors and sometimes casting whites in redface.[24]

This is where my history gets personal, for I grew up in Provo in the 1970s. My father was a BYU professor; my mother was a ward organist and a caregiver to her elderly parents. Immediately before moving to Provo as retirees, my maternal grandparents served as missionaries to the Southwest Indian Mission (Arizona and New Mexico), where they did their best to "reactivate" lapsed converts. A Church handbook from the era described proselytizing to Lamanites in terms of "integration and assimilation" and noted the power of music: "Perhaps no other race of people loves to sing more than do the Indians." It instructed missionaries to "take advantage of this native talent and desire" by distributing songbooks and teaching the "songs of Zion."[25] In July 1969, my grandfather helped with "gathering up" Diné girls and boys in pickup trucks to take them to the high school auditorium in Fort Wingate, New Mexico, to rehearse Mutual Improvement Association (MIA) and Primary songs, including "I Am a Child of God," for an upcoming pageant in the multi-purpose "cultural hall" (a basketball court with a stage):

I am a child of God.
Rich blessings are in store;
If I but learn to do his will,
I'll live with him once more.

Lead me, guide me, walk beside me,
Help me find the way.
Teach me all that I must do
To live with him someday.[26]

According to my grandmother's diary, most of the "cast" failed to show up at performance time because the pageant competed with a tribal dance event the same day.[27]

In Provo, Native students at BYU formed middle-of-the-road music groups such as the Lamanite Generation. I remember attending their performances on campus. My grandfather owned an LP called *Go, My Son* (1967); the title track by Arliene Nofchissey Williams (Diné) and Carnes Burson (mixed ancestry, including Ute) was the signature song of the Lamanite Generation. President Kimball received many such discs as gifts. But unlike the Osmonds, the Lamanite Generation never got a chance to sing in the Tabernacle. In 1971, the fourth and final All-Lamanite Youth Conference took place at the Salt Palace Convention Center, with an associated "Lamanite Extravaganza" held in the Valley Music Hall. Following this Saturday night musical "variety show," which included "Go, My Son," the Indigenous MIA Mormons were invited to the Tabernacle on Sunday morning to sit silently and listen reverently to *Music and the Spoken Word*.[28]

Members of the American Indian Movement (AIM) could be more vocal at Temple Square: they demonstrated outside the gates—heavily monitored by police—during General Conference at least three times in the early 1970s. In 1974, they issued a list of "challenges" to the Church, including the repatriation of skulls and bones on display in the Temple Square museum. As for the Church's vaunted Indian programs, AIM field director Vernon Bellecourt (White Earth Band of the Minnesota Chippewa Tribe) characterized them as "acts of cultural and religious genocide." AIM emulated the NAACP, which had in the 1960s protested at Temple Square and the adjacent Administrative Block over the Church's "silence" regarding civil rights.[29]

After Kimball's death in 1985, the LDS Church—following the lead of Boyd K. Packer—abruptly dropped its outreach to tribal nations of the Intermountain West and redoubled its efforts to internationalize through color-blind conversion, particularly in Mexico. Even while downplaying the theology of lineage, the Church and its apologists encouraged a geographic reorientation of the Book of Mormon from North America to Central America.[30] Energies once channeled into assimilation programs and music festivals were redirected into a global missionary apparatus, service in which became all but compulsory for young men during the 1970s and 1980s. The LDS conversion rate reached an all-time high in 1990—and has plummeted since, though not for lack of effort. Through two-year missions to foreign countries, Gen-X Utah Mormons became less parochial in the religious sense (if no less imperial in the geopolitical sense). The "mountain home" era of ethnic regionalism dissipated.[31]

The symbolic end date for Mormonism as an ethnicity is 1980, when the LDS Church instituted the "consolidated schedule," meaning that each ward met once a week in a three-hour "block" rather than holding separate auxiliary meetings throughout the week. Mormon families—including women in their designated role as housewives—could now spend more time at home, making music at "Family Home Evening" under the authority of the priesthood-holding husband. Accompanying these temporal and spatial shifts were financial and organizational changes that created greater uniformity and equity among wards but also less variety, not to mention fewer opportunities for congregational singing and less demand for organists and choristers. In 1985, when a revised international version of the hymnal came out, the green-cover volume still included a few hymns written for four-part chorus and a few more for men's chorus, notated in the tenor clef. But most Latter-day Saints in Utah, the former "Zion," could no longer sing them, and they ignored those numbers in favor of easier ones, which they—like converts in Mexico and Brazil—began to sing in unison.[32]

Consolidation affected children's music most of all. Moving Primary from Wednesday to Sunday required a repertoire that was more "reverent" and gospel-focused. A new songbook was authorized for that reason. A simplification of harmonies, rhythms, and arrangements accompanied a complexification of lyrics. These rhyming words emphasized doctrine and also orthopraxy: quietude, stillness, order, cleanliness, grooming. Prior to mid-century, LDS children's songs about reverence had not existed. *Sing with Me* (1974) included "Father, I Will Reverent Be," "I Will Try to Be Reverent," and "Reverently, Quietly"—a placid culmination to the tenure of LaVern Watts Parmley, who had served as general president of the Primary from 1951 to 1974 and had instituted weekly "reverence programs."[33] *Children's Songbook* (1989), the post-consolidation edition, retained the Parmley didacticisms and piled on more: "I Want to Be Reverent," "Reverence Is Love," and "We Are Reverent."[34]

Although the new songbook was less playful, it did keep "Book of Mormon Stories," a thumping song—a cringey example of "Indianist music"—about Lamanites in "ancient history." Increasingly, Lamanites in the theological present did not exist. Whereas Latter-day Saints of the mid-nineteenth century had sung charismatically in ancient Amerindian languages, I and other LDS children of the late twentieth century did the churchly equivalent of the tomahawk chop, "playing Indian" in Primary on Sundays. That irreverent act, like LDS reverence itself, was further proof of whiteness.[35]

NOTES

1   "Marketing the Mormon Image: An Interview with Melvin J. Ashton," *Dialogue* 10.3 (Spring 1977): 15–20, statistic on 16.

2   See Mark Porcaro, "'We Have Something Really Going between Us Now': Columbia Records' Influence on the Repertoire of the Mormon Tabernacle Choir, 1949–1992," *Choral Scholar* 1.1 (Spring 2009): 41–115.

3   Richard L. Evans Jr., *Richard L. Evans: The Man and the Message* (Salt Lake City: Bookcraft, 1973), 84–85; "Richard L. Evans of the 'Spoken Word,'" *Deseret News*, November 1, 1971. The intimate conversational voice of Presbyterian minister Fred Rogers may be considered the successor to Evans's voice in US popular culture; *Mister Rogers' Neighborhood* ran on public television from 1968 to 2001. Across the twentieth century, the slow, soft vocal style shared by both men became generally more appropriate for children than for adults.

4   Matt Stone and Trey Parker, interviewed by Terry Gross on *Fresh Air*, WHYY, distributed by NPR, May 9, 2011. For context, see Jared Farmer, "Why *The Book of Mormon* (the Musical) Is Awesomely Lame," *Religious Dispatches*, June 13, 2011; Michael Hicks, "Elder Price Superstar," in *Spencer Kimball's Record Collection*, 177–186. On the queerness of "Mormon" vocality on Broadway, see Johnson, *Mormons, Musical Theater, and Belonging in America*.

5   See Josh Kun, *Audiotopia: Music, Race, and America* (Berkeley: University of California Press, 2005); Karl Hagstrom Miller, *Segregating Sound: Inventing Folk and Pop Music in the Age of Jim Crow* (Durham, NC: Duke University Press, 2010); Jennifer Lynn Stoever,

The Sonic Color Line: Race and the Cultural Politics of Listening (New York: NYU Press, 2016); Nina Sun Eidsheim, *The Race of Sound: Listening, Timbre, and Vocality in African American Music* (Durham, NC: Duke University Press, 2019).

6   This is a play on "acousmatic blackness," a term from Mendi Obadike; "Low Fidelity: Stereotyped Blackness in the Field of Sound" (PhD dissertation, Duke University, Durham, NC, 2005).

7   See Connor Sheldon Kenaston, "Faith Networks: National Broadcasting and the Making of American Religion" (PhD dissertation, University of Virginia, Charlottesville, 2022), 121–154; Madalin Olivia Trigg Price, "'Wings over Jordan' and American Radio: 1937–1947" (PhD dissertation, University of Southern Mississippi, Hattiesburg, 1995).

8   Cornwall, *Century of Singing*, 408.

9   *Songs of the North and South, 1861–1865* (Columbia Masterworks, 1961).

10   *General Handbook of Instructions* 18 (1960), 25.

11   "Contralto Arrives for Concert," *Deseret News*, April 28, 1937.

12   Elva Plummer, interviewed by Winnifred Margetts, January 13, 1989, Everett L. Cooley Oral History Project, Marriott Library, University of Utah, 43–46.

13   Roy Wilkins with Tom Matthews, *Standing Fast: The Autobiography of Roy Wilkins* (New York: Viking, 1982), 183–184. For context, see Wallace R. Bennett, "The Negro in Utah," *Utah Law Review* 3.3 (Spring 195): 340–348. In the railroad era, Ogden, not Salt Lake City, was the center of Black life in Utah.

14   "'Ave Maria' Will Be an Encore," *Salt Lake Tribune*, March 19, 1948; "Famous Contralto Had to Use Freight Lift in Hotel Utah," *Salt Lake Tribune*, April 9, 1993.

15   See Matthew L. Harris, *Second-Class Saints: Black Mormons and the Struggle for Racial Equality* (New York: Oxford University Press, 2024), 93–126; Susan Peterson, "The Great and Dreadful Day: Mormon Folklore of the Apocalypse," *Utah Historical Quarterly* 44.4 (Fall 1976): 365–378; "Rumors Prompt Police Alert in 4 Locations," *Salt Lake Tribune*, August 7, 1967.

16   Ezra Taft Benson, untitled talk, *One Hundred Thirty-Seventh Semi-Annual Conference* (Salt Lake City: LDS Church, 1967), 34–39.

17   "Music Department subject and correspondence files, 1919–1973," CR 108-10, box 4, fd. 3, Church History Library (CHL).

18   McKay identified the applicant only as "a Negro woman"; see Harvard S. Heath, ed., *Confidence amid Change: The Presidential Diaries of David O. McKay, 1951–1970* (Salt Lake City: Signature Books, 2019), 717–718. Hugh B. Brown, first counselor to McKay from 1963 to 1970, was the most notable exception to the apostolic record of racism.

19   See Joanna Brooks, *Mormonism and White Supremacy: American Religion and the Problem of Racial Innocence* (New York: Oxford University Press, 2020), 85–110. For context on the ultraconservative LDS turn, see Matthew L. Harris, ed., *Thunder from the Right: Ezra Taft Benson in Mormonism and Politics* (Urbana: University of Illinois Press, 2019); Matthew L. Harris, *Watchman on the Tower: Ezra Taft Benson and the Making of the Mormon Right* (Urbana: University of Illinois Press, 2020).

20   See Wynetta Willis Martin, *Black Mormon Tells Her Story: "The Truth Sang Louder than My Position"* (Salt Lake City: Hawkes, 1972), quotes on 38–39, 73. According to the memoir, Martin was hired as BYU's first Black instructor (in nursing). See Laura L. Bush,

Faithful Transgressions in the American West: Six Twentieth-Century Mormon Women's Autobiographical Acts (Logan: Utah State University Press, 2004), 109–144.

21   Quote from UPI story, "Black Priesthood Advocate Banned by Court from Conference," *Daily Herald* (Provo), September 29, 1976. For immediate context, see Edward L. Kimball, "Spencer W. Kimball and the Revelation on Priesthood," *BYU Studies* 47.2 (2008): 4–78; Harris, *Second-Class Saints*, 192–226. For general context, see Newell G. Bringhurst, *Saints, Slaves, and Blacks: The Changing Place of Black People within Mormonism* (Westport, CT: Greenwood, 1981); Russell W. Stevenson, *For the Cause of Righteousness: A Global History of Blacks and Mormonism, 1830–2013* (Salt Lake City: Greg Kofford Books, 2014).

22   The interview can be found on YouTube.

23   All the quotes in this paragraph are from Official Declaration 2. See also Harris, *Second-Class Saints*, 227–257. The revelation did not end the Church's antipathy toward interracial marriage, nor did it end LDS theological racism.

24   See Armand L. Mauss, *All Abraham's Children: Changing Mormon Conceptions of Race and Lineage* (Urbana: University of Illinois Press, 2003); Brandon Morgan, "Educating the Lamanites: A Brief History of the LDS Indian Student Placement Program," *Journal of Mormon History* 35.4 (Fall 2009): 191–217; Scott C. Esplin "'You Can Make Your Own Bright Future, Tom Trails': Evaluating the Impact of the LDS Indian Seminary Program," *Journal of Mormon History* 42.4 (October 2016): 172–207; Matthew Garrett, *Making Lamanites: Mormons, Native Americans, and the Indian Student Placement Program, 1947–2000* (Salt Lake City: University of Utah Press, 2016); R. Warren Metcalf, "'Which Side of the Line?' American Indian Students and Programs at Brigham Young University, 1960–1983," in *Essays on American Indian and Mormon History*, ed. Brenden W. Rensink and P. Jane Hafen (Salt Lake City: University of Utah Press, 2019), 225–245; Hicks, *Spencer Kimball's Record Collection* (title essay). The prophetic phrase "they shall be a white and a delightsome people" comes from the original 1830 edition of the Book of Mormon, 2 Nephi 30:6.

25   "Missionary Handbook for Lamanite Missionaries" (undated), M256.4 M678, CHL, 1, 11.

26   This is the third verse (with chorus) from the 1957 song, with words by Naomi Ward Randall and music by Mildred Tanner Petit.

27   *Diary of Lela W. Clark*, 320–321.

28   I read coverage of the event in the *Deseret News* and the *Salt Lake Tribune*, April–May 1971, at Utah Digital Newspapers: https://digitalnewspapers.org. That Sunday turned out to be one of Richard Evans's final spoken word performances.

29   "Indians Give LDS 7 'Challenges,'" *Salt Lake Tribune*, April 8, 1974. For context, see Max Perry Mueller, "The Pageantry of Protest in Temple Square," in *Out of Obscurity: Mormonism since 1945*, ed. Patrick Q. Mason and John G. Turner (New York: Oxford University Press, 2016), 123–143.

30   In the twenty-first century, DNA evidence presented a new challenge to historicist claims about the Book of Mormon; see Thomas W. Murphy, "Lamanite Genesis, Genealogy, and Genetics," in *American Apocrypha: Essays on the* Book of the Mormon, ed. Dan Vogel and Brent Lee Metcalfe (Salt Lake City: Signature Books, 2002), 47–77; Simon Southerton, *Losing a Lost Tribe: Native Americans, DNA, and the Mormon Church* (Salt Lake City: Signature Books, 2004).

31 See Gina Colvin and Joanna Brooks, eds., *Decolonizing Mormonism: Approaching a Postcolonial Zion* (Salt Lake City: University of Utah Press, 2018); R. Gordon Shepherd, A. Gary Shepherd, and Ryan T. Cragun, eds., *The Palgrave Handbook of Global Mormonism* (Cham, Switzerland: Palgrave, 2020).

32 For context on ward singing in the late twentieth century, see Paul C. Pollei, "The Decline of Music in Mormon Culture," *Sunstone* 16.3 (September 1992): 11–14; Emily Spencer, "Why Mormons Sing in Parts (Or Don't)," *Dialogue* 48.4 (Winter 2015): 45–67; Michael Hicks, "How to Make (and Unmake) a Mormon Hymnbook," in *A Firm Foundation: Church Organization and Administration*, ed. David J. Whittaker and Arnold K. Garr (Salt Lake City: Deseret Book, 2011), 502–519.

33 See Carol Cornwall Madsen and Susan Staker Oman, *Sisters and Little Saints: One Hundred Years of Primary* (Salt Lake City: Deseret Books, 1979); LaVern Parmley, interviewed by Jill Mulvay, Salt Lake City, 1974–1976, OH 296, CHL, esp. 124–129.

34 See Kristine Haglund Harris, "'Who Shall Sing if Not the Children?' Primary Songbooks, 1880–1989," *Dialogue* 37.4 (Winter 2004): 90–127; Colleen Jillian Karnas-Haines, "The Church of Jesus Christ of Latter-day Saints/Mormon Children's Music: Its History, Transmission, and Place in Children's Cognitive Development" (PhD dissertation, University of Maryland, College Park, 2005).

35 For context, see Philip J. Deloria, *Playing Indian* (New Haven, CT: Yale University Press, 1998); Michael V. Pisani, *Imagining Native America in Music* (New Haven, CT: Yale University Press, 2005); Farmer, *On Zion's Mount*, 328–378. On terminology, see John-Charles Duffy, "The Use of 'Lamanite' in Official LDS Discourse," *Journal of Mormon History* 34.1 (Winter 2008): 118–167.

9
GLOBAL MEDIA, INC.

If Mormonism *was* media from its beginning, the Corporation of the President of The Church of Jesus Christ of Latter-day Saints *became* global media in the era of Gordon B. Hinckley. He was the definition of a company man. After starting as the Church's first publicity staffer in 1935, Hinckley worked his way up the ladder on both the business and prophetic sides, becoming president in 1995. During the middle decades of the century, when Mormons began erecting temples in foreign countries, Hinckley was in charge of the sensitive assignment of adapting and translating the "endowment" (a ceremony that includes a sacred play, historically performed with live actors) into a movie dubbed in non-English languages. Hinckley also became a leading figure at Bonneville International, the Church-owned media corporation founded in 1964—itself a subsidiary of Deseret Management Corporation, the operating company that handled for-profit entities of the tax-exempt religious organization. Bonneville acquired a portfolio of thirteen commercial radio stations as well as KSL-TV. As the Church became wealthy for the first time, it built more and more temples and chapels with movie theaters, and installed extra-large satellite dishes at regional "stake centers" so congregants could watch transmissions from the Tabernacle.[1]

Consistently across the twentieth century, the LDS Church—like other conservative Christian religions—was an early adopter of new media. But technological enthusiasm was always laced with moral worry. Ezra Taft Benson described a paradox: "The inventors of these wonders were inspired by the Lord. But once their good works were introduced to the world, the powers of darkness began to employ them for our destruction."[2] The same technology that allowed worthy Saints to watch a sacred film in the holy temple allowed young Mormons to watch sexually explicit

https://doi.org/10.5876/781646427031.c009

content in the movie theater. Similarly, once the internet arrived, Latter-day Saints celebrated their new ability to advance Heavenly Father's imperative to do genealogy while warning about the Adversary's new ability to spread pornography.[3]

In regard to music, the sacred possibilities and profane dangers of media players came back to the fore with the advent of the Sony Walkman in 1979. Young people could be enveloped in loudness without parental knowledge. But at the discretion of the mission president, missionaries on their two-year isolation from family and mass media could listen to wholesome cassettes—including home recordings of family voices. During the 1980s, the Church responded to the media moment by producing taped narrations of LDS scriptures and also "Especially for Youth" (EFY) cassette tapes with Church-approved pop music. A group of composers, most notably Janice Kapp Perry, developed a genre of LDS ballad—just shy of Christian pop, following the model of *Saturday's Warrior*—that could be appropriate for missionary listening despite being inappropriate for sacrament meeting. Many mission presidents developed listening rules ("EFY only," "classical only," "MoTab only"), though these were hard to enforce. Because the Mormon Tabernacle Choir made albums that contained Disney and Broadway tunes, some missionaries took license to broadly interpret the listening rules. The religious import of the choir's playlists and discography was a point of persistent confusion for Church members in the last quarter of the twentieth century.[4]

After CBS/Columbia (through its new parent company, Sony) ended its long recording relationship with the LDS Church in 1987, the choir wandered from label to label. The impetus for the final breakup (with Telarc) was a contract dispute over compensation. According to union rules governing the recording of orchestral musicians, the Church needed to pay its Orchestra at Temple Square, a newish volunteer organization. Unlike the Tabernacle organists—professionals who paid dues to the American Federation of Musicians as well as tithes to the Church—the members of the orchestra (like the choir) were volunteers. Instead of paying them to record, the Church simply formed its own label, another subsidiary of Bonneville International, in 2001. Around the same time, the Church founded Intellectual Reserve, Inc., to handle its intellectual property assets in accordance with a Joseph Smith revelation from 1830, in the voice of the Lord, to "do my work in this thing yea even in securing the Copy right & they shall do it with an eye single to my Glory that it may be the means of bringing souls unto Salvation."[5] Thanks to the financial success of Ensign Peak Advisors—an investment management auxiliary hived off in 1997—the Brethren had the capacity to go independent in almost all forms of media. In the twenty-first century, the Tabernacle roster mostly made music for internal consumption by Church members. Organ and choral music were no longer touchstones of Americana, and many large-market TV and radio stations had dropped *Music and the Spoken Word*.[6]

Freed from commercial obligations, the choir's repertoire reverted to something more like that of Evans Stephens, the original court composer at the Tabernacle. A new era of "home music" ensued under the successive directorships of Craig D. Jessop and especially Mack Wilberg. "The Tabernacle Choir does not exist for art," said Jessop, candidly. "We have chosen the musical art as an expression of our faith."[7] Enhanced by the orchestra, the choir's radio program became an ecumenical version of the Boston Pops. The new LDS anthemic style of light classical music—the sacred pops—was strongly influenced by British composer John Rutter. (Not coincidentally, Jessop had served a stint with Rutter's Cambridge Singers.) But the sound of the Tabernacle—giant chorus with full orchestra, yet never exactly loud—was still distinctively Mormon. Wilberg's prolific composing and arranging allowed the choir to sing fresh material without dipping into contemporary praise and worship music. His MoTab did not sway. It persisted with neo-Romantic chorales rooted in English Protestant hymnody and US folksong.

Through the mediatization of the Church corporation, the choir even entered the Holy of Holies. Originally multi-purpose acoustic spaces, LDS temples became paragons of sacred silence in the mid-twentieth century, only to transform into venues for Muzak-like ambient music.[8] By the late twentieth century, it was common to hear an electronic organ or tapes of the Tabernacle Choir piped into temple anterooms. The ritual rooms—the spaces used after the sacred temple play—and the concluding Celestial Room (a space for prayerful reflection) remained entirely free of music. But what about the movie theater? Once the Church had turned its sacred play into cinema, the media format by convention demanded a soundtrack. That arrived in 1988 with a commissioned score by Kurt Bestor, a Mormon whose composing career had begun with advertising jingles. Leading LDS music historian Michael Hicks detected echoes of *Star Trek* in Bestor's "Hollywood-style" score.[9] Notably, the film included a wordless choir over which heavenly voices spoke in acousmatic whiteness, a bit like Richard Evans speaking over the humming of the Tabernacle Choir. To record Bestor's celestial chorus, the Church chose a select group of choir members. The convention of the wordless choir began in nineteenth-century opera and appeared prominently in Debussy's *Nocturnes*, Ravel's *Daphnis and Chloë*, and Holst's *The Planets*. It migrated to film media in the 1920s, as featured in Hollywood scores by leading figures such as Max Steiner, Erich Korngold, Hugo Friedhofer, and Miklós Rózsa. By mid-century it was a cinematic cliché to use a wordless female chorus to signal epiphany, mystery, awe, the numinous, or the divine.[10]

Contemporary temples are not acoustic spaces, and neither is the Conference Center—the stone-clad megachurch just north of Temple Square that has obviated the Tabernacle as the gathering space for General Conference. This building was the dream of President Gordon B. Hinckley and the culmination of his career in media. It was built to last "at least 150 years," or, as Hinckley put it, "for as long as the earth lasts."[11] The vast central hall, with its curving, cantilevered balconies, was designed (unlike the Tabernacle) to the dictates of electric transmission and amplification, with the best speaker-delay system money could buy. Its 21,000 seats—all with unobstructed views of the podium—made it the largest theater auditorium in the world. The building has one primary purpose: to accommodate as many believers as possible in one room to see and hear the prophet. The facility includes sixty soundproof booths so non-Anglophones can benefit from simultaneous language translations.

The original plans for the Conference Center didn't call for an organ. Tabernacle organist John Longhurst rallied enough support to make it happen but, in typical LDS fashion, the Church took money from the volunteer choir's discretionary fund to subsidize the instrument. Despite the size and grandeur of the organ, built by Schoenstein & Co. with casing by Fetzers' Inc., it has not become iconic like the even larger Tabernacle

Organ. The arched wooden roof above the 7,708 pipes directs the sound forward, yet the instrument still sounds small in the cavernous space, with all the upholstered seats and carpet swallowing its sound. (Needless to say, a pin-drop test would fail.) Because the organ was not completed in time for the building's dedication in April 2000, sound technicians piped in an electronic keyboard, using the Schoenstein pipes as a facade. The audience may not have noticed—the big event at that General Conference was a Hosanna Shout. When President Hinckley led the triple cheer to dedicate the building, the spectacle of 21,000 people waving white handkerchiefs was more impressive than the volume of their shouting in unison.[12]

An underlying scientific principle accounts for some of this. As measured by acousticians, there is a point of diminishing returns with the size of a vocal group. Counterintuitively, a choir with 300 singers will be barely louder, as measured in decibels, than a choir of 50 singers, assuming they are singing the same way. The sound level of a choir increases by merely three decibels for each doubling in size. As choral music enthusiasts know, a small Slavic chorus can generate more sonic intensity than the entire Tabernacle Choir. The reasons are vocal resonance, vocal intensity, vocal spacing, and vocal blending. A handful of professional singers, widely spaced, singing in a less blended way will be experienced as much louder than a bevy of less resonant amateurs, closely spaced, singing with a more blended or homogeneous tone.[13]

An underlying cultural condition matters just as much. Post-correlation Latter-day Saints never pull out all the stops. The Schoenstein organ shares some similarities with a modern prophet: both have "voices" or "registers," and both have the potential to make the noise of many waters, but mostly they make moderate sounds. Sforzando is not a musical, behavioral, or organizational option—except in the setting of BYU football home games, when LaVell Edwards Stadium in Provo quakes and thunders. In religious settings, though, the sonic (and sartorial) spectrum available to Latter-day Saints is quite narrow, which leads to characteristic sound effects: shushed babies, mumbled prayers, muffled tears, suppressed laughs, passive-aggressive pauses. Emblematically, the Tabernacle Choir at Temple Square (its revised name since 2018) has achieved a big sound without loudness. Its intensity ranges from mezzo forte to forte. Molto pianissimo is technically unachievable with amateurs, and molto fortissimo is culturally impermissible for Mormons. The 300 men and women in suits and dresses convey a sound of collective restraint. Religiously, the combined voice of the volunteer choir is more important than the solo voice of the trained singer. Likewise, the corporate voice of the Brethren is more important than the single voice of any particular prophet since the singular Joseph Smith.

These cultural conditions affect musical taste. Back in 1914, Evan Stephens described "Mormonistic" music using these adjectives: light, bright, optimistic, joyful, active, earnest, clean, natural.[14] Remarkably, most of those descriptors still apply to the selections broadcast from the Tabernacle and the Conference Center. Depending on the listener's taste, the sound is sweet, soothing, uplifting, timeless—or syrupy, corny, cheesy, old-timey. It could easily become camp if Mormons were ironic, flamboyant, or soulful, but they tend to be the opposite—sincerely temperate. LDS broadcast music can also be described by absences: of virtuosity, improvisation, minor modes (with 99.9 percent of the songs in the 1985 hymnal in a major key), unresolved dissonance, atonality, microtonality, feedback, polyrhythm, fast rhythm, quintuple meter, heavy percussion, high volume, wide tonal shifts, rapid beats per minute. Since the 1960s, Church leaders have specifically told teens and missionaries to listen to moderate and modest music and to shun loudness and intensity.[15] According to Spotify user data, BYU students have the "lowest energy music taste in the world."[16] The culture is non-caffeinated.

When recording legend Gladys Knight, the "Empress of Soul," converted to Mormonism in 1997, she experienced culture shock. "She once told me that she enjoyed everything about this Church except the music," said a lighthearted Hinckley, when introducing Sister Knight for her performance with the choir at his ninetieth birthday celebration in the Conference Center. She gently ribbed the prophet in reply: "If it is OK with you I would like to clarify something. I love the music of this church as I love this church. It is just that I knew when I came I may have a little withdrawal, because of the foot stomping and hand clapping that I am used to." Afterward, Knight commented on her solo with the Tabernacle Choir: "My heart is happy, because we met in the middle tonight."[17]

From one perspective, the continuity of a distinctively "Mormon" broadcast sound is good brand maintenance. However, in today's hyper-sorted media environment, the middlebrow music of the LDS Church—as represented by the Tabernacle Choir—may be more of a PR drag than a lift. By the time President Ronald Reagan gave a shout-out to "America's Choir," the ensemble had effectively become White America's Choir or (to use an anachronism) the Red States' Choir. No one could miss the symbolism of Barack Obama, defeater of GOP standard-bearer and LDS scion Mitt Romney, choosing the Brooklyn Tabernacle Choir to sing the "Battle Hymn of the Republic" at his second inaugural. Likewise, no one could miss the import of the Salt Lake choir accepting the controversial invitation from Donald Trump to perform at his inauguration four years later. Many Americans who remembered the racist priesthood ban now equated MoTab with MAGA.[18]

In terms of membership as well as style, the choir's continuing "white bread" quality is largely a function of its location in Utah and does not reflect the overall demographics of Mormondom—or, for that matter, of the Beehive State. If the LDS Church is no longer the "fastest growing church," Utah was in fact the fastest-growing US state between 2010 and 2020, largely due to in-migration, with 62 percent of the population in the last census defined as "white alone, not Hispanic or Latino." The LDS share of Utah's population peaked at 77 percent in 1990 and fell to roughly 60 percent by 2020—or closer to 40 percent if you counted only those who self-identified as LDS, which excluded many thousands of baptized but anything-but-active Millennials and Gen-Zers. If not yet a worldwide religion, Mormonism is now composed of "multiple Zions"—notably the United States, Mexico, Brazil, the Philippines, and the Pacific Islands—with a self-reported (inflated) total membership of roughly 17 million, which is larger than the number of Jehovah's Witnesses but smaller than a single mega-city such as São Paulo.[19]

Things change, even in organizations run by ninety-somethings. To belatedly address the mismatch between its white legacy media and its non-white recent converts, the Church in 2022 started producing a parallel Spanish-language version of *Music and the Spoken Word* with a rotating cast of announcers, including a woman, Garna Mejia, in the role of Richard Evans. The YouTube advertisement for *Música y Palabras de Inspiración* featured the English-language choir—with its signature white timbre—singing a lightly syncopated Latin American tune. Even this was noteworthy: during the Priesthood Correlation era, syncopation had been categorically banned from LDS Church broadcasting. Additional changes are in the air. As announced in April 2024, the choir in its General Conference appearances will henceforth include international guests from its "Global Participant Program."[20]

Simultaneously, the Church began field-testing songs from the forthcoming and long-anticipated *Hymns—for Home and Church*, one consolidated songbook for an international religion, with editions expected in more than fifty languages. Two of the early additions were gospel tunes, "His Eye Is on the Sparrow" and "It Is Well with My Soul." Accompanying this landmark project was a revision to the 2022 *Handbook of Instructions* that eliminated the Clark-McKay discouragement of any instruments except organ in church meetings. The "hymn-only" guidance for organ prelude music had already been relaxed. As of now, judgment calls on musical reverence are left to the discretion of local bishops, informed by cultural context. All in all, Latter-day Saints are beginning to experiment with the kind of musical accommodation Catholics made after Vatican II. Ironically, though, there are fewer opportunities to make churchly music, at least in congregations. As of 2018, the Sunday "block" service went down to two hours, a reduction from the three-hour block instituted in 1980. As part of the Church's stand on the "traditional family," General Authorities encouraged domestic music making in a "home-centered" Church.

In sacrament meetings at Utah's powerhouse wards, brass and string ensembles playing tasteful hymn arrangements now seem to be the order of the day. If the new policy continues, drums may eventually appear in African branch services and guitars and accordions in Latin American stake conferences. It still seems unlikely, however, that US Mormons will give in to euphoric singing and swaying or that the Tabernacle Choir at Temple Square will sound like the Brooklyn Tabernacle Choir. The quest for restrained white respectability—an overreaction to the gauntlet of humiliation Latter-day Saints once endured—become internalized long ago.

Mormons call this stance "quiet dignity." They say "amen," not "*Amen!*" Despite the rapprochement between the LDS Church and the Southern Baptist Convention over race and especially gender (including die-on-that-hill resistance to LGBT people in religion), Mormons do not want to be confused with evangelicals; and they especially do not want to be linked to Pentecostals, who started—in interracial fashion—speaking and signing in tongues in the first decade of the twentieth century, even as LDS leaders narrowed the proper use of this spiritual gift to xenoglossia in the context of foreign-language missions.[21]

Given this legacy, it was a signal event when Gladys Knight performed "Love One Another" with a gospel choir in the Salt Lake Tabernacle, accompanied by a portable electronic jazz organ—not the pipe organ—to mark the fortieth anniversary (2018) of the revelation that ended the priesthood and temple bans. The LDS Church billed this special evening of music and the spoken word as a "celebration" when *truth and reconciliation* or *repentance and forgiveness* would have been more apposite choices. Knight's emotive performance, which sounded unmistakably Black in timbral style, was a historic departure for the Tabernacle—the kind of audition that Evan Stephens, Heber J. Grant, Tracy Y. Cannon, J. Reuben Clark, and other architects of the Mormon sound of music would have disliked. Knight had previously won a Grammy for Best Gospel Choir or Chorus Album for *One Voice* (2005), a collection that included LDS standards "Come, Come, Ye Saints" and "I Am a Child of God."

Two years after this "Be One" celebration, the First Presidency marked the bicentennial of the First Vision. Nineteenth-century Latter-day Saints could not have anticipated this milestone, for they had expected an imminent Second Coming.[22] April 2020, the designated anniversary, happened to coincide with the strict period of Covid-19 lockdown, so the prophet, Russell M. Nelson, presided remotely from an audience-free Conference Center, with only select Brethren and audiovisual technicians in the hall. Nelson proceeded with his plan to lead a Hosanna Shout to mark 200 years of vicarious theophany through the voices of living prophets.[23] Watching on their phones, tablets, computers, or flat-screen TVs, believers witnessed the ninety-five-year-old revelator weakly wave a handkerchief while unemphatically uttering the ceremonial phrase. His sound was a simulacrum of a shout. Whether the virtual audience at home synchronously shouted "to God and the Lamb" with reverent intensity and millenarian joy I cannot know for sure, but I can make an educated guess based on observations of awkward airings at recent US temple dedications.

Utah Saints long ago lost the ecstatic register. It could be found again, perhaps, through the charity of the Church's future majority for whom Zion is not mountain home.

NOTES

1 See Herbert F. Murray, "A Half Century of Broadcasting in the Church," *Ensign* 2.8 (August 1972): 48–51; Fred C. Esplin, "The Church as Broadcaster," *Dialogue* 10.3 (Spring 1977): 25–45; for contemporary context, Robert Gottlieb and Peter Wiley, *America's Saints: The Rise of Mormon Power* (New York: Putnam's Sons, 1984); John Heinerman and Anson D. Shupe, *The Mormon Corporate Empire* (Boston: Beacon, 1985).

2 Ezra Taft Benson, "Satan's Thrust," *Ensign* 1.12 (December 1971): 53–56, quote on 56.

3 See Feller, *Eternity in the Ether*, 125–140.

4 I researched missionary experiences by reading Reddit forums. On EFY, see John G. Bytheway, "A History of 'Especially for Youth,' 1976–1986" (MA thesis, Brigham Young University, Provo, 2003).

5 John Whitmer, scribe, "Revelation, circa Early 1830," Revelation Book 1, in *The Joseph Smith Papers: Documents*, vol. 1: *July 1828–June 1831*, ed. Michael Hubbard MacKay, Gerrit J. Dirkmaat, Grant Underwood, Robert J. Woodford, and William G. Hartley (Salt Lake City: Church Historian's Press, 2013), 108–112; also available at josephsmithpapers.org.

6 The most recent broadcasting figure for *Music and the Spoken Word*, provided by the LDS Church Newsroom in 2020, is "more than 2,000 media stations," though I cannot verify that; moreover, in a time of media fragmentation, the number of outlets is no longer a good indicator of total viewers and listeners.

7 Jessop quoted in Mark David Porcaro, "The Secularization of the Repertoire of the Mormon Tabernacle Choir, 1949–1992" (PhD dissertation, University of North Carolina, Chapel Hill, 2006), 173.

8 Ironically, the best place in late twentieth-century Mormondom to hear perfect silence was not any temple but the anechoic chamber at BYU built by Harvey Fletcher in his retirement years.

9 Hicks, *Mormon Tabernacle Choir*, 152.

10 See Philip Daniel Nauman, "*Sirènes, Spectres, Ombres*: Dramatic Vocalization in the Nineteenth and Twentieth Centuries" (PhD dissertation, Boston University, Boston, MA, 2009). Bestor subsequently wrote a second soundtrack for the endowment film; according to many people, including commenters on Reddit, his music for the Creation plagiarized "Cadillac of the Skies" from John Williams's score to Steven Spielberg's *Empire of the Sun* (1987).

11 "The Conference Center: 'This New and Wonderful Hall,'" *Ensign* 30.10 (October 2000): 32–41, quotes on 36.

12 See John Longhurst, *Magnum Opus: The Building of the Schoenstein Organ at the Conference Center of The Church of Jesus Christ of Latter-day Saints* (Salt Lake City: Intellectual Reserve, 2009).

13 Ingo R. Titze and Lynn Maxfield, "Acoustic Factors Affecting the Dynamic Range of a Choir," *Journal of the Acoustical Society of America* 142.4 (October 2017): 2464–2468.

14 Stephens, "Songs and Music of the Latter-day Saints."

15 See the various editions of the booklet *For the Strength of Youth* (1965–present) available at CHL. For context, see Brent D. Fillmore, "Promoting Peculiarity—Different Editions of *For the Strength of Youth*," *Religious Educator* 8.3 (2007): 75–88.

16 Emma Everett Johnson, "BYU Students Have Lowest Energy Music Taste in the World, Spotify Data Finds," *Daily Universe*, February 2, 2023. There are exceptions: the music group Imagine Dragons got its start in Provo; and far more BYU students have listened to the up-tempo MOR band the Killers (fronted by Mormon celebrity Brandon Flowers) than to the "slowcore" indie band Low (composed of LDS couple Alan Sparhawk and Mimi Parker).

17 Sarah Jane Weaver, "An Evening of Celebration," *Church News*, July 1, 2000, 3, 6.

18 See Max Perry Mueller, " 'Not My Choir,' " *Slate*, January 9, 2017; Brooks, *Mormonism and White Supremacy*. The choir has twice performed at the BYU-hosted "Stadium of Fire," a Fourth of July patriotic spectacular broadcast on the American Forces Network, part of Provo's annual "America's Freedom Festival."

19 For past Church-reported statistics, see the *Deseret News Church Almanac*, published biennially from 1974 to 2013. On recent trends, see Jana Riess, *The Next Mormons: How Millennials Are Changing the LDS Church* (New York: Oxford University Press, 2019); R. Gordon Shepherd, A. Gary Shepherd, and Ryan T. Cragun, eds., *The Palgrave Handbook of Global Mormonism* (Cham, Switzerland: Palgrave, 2020). The once-touted projection by sociologist Rodney Stark (made in 1984) of 60 to 265 million Latter-day Saints in 2080 now seems implausible.

20 This kind of global outreach had prophet-approved precedent; see Judd Case, "Sounds from the Center: Liriel's Performance and Ritual Pilgrimage," *Journal of Media and Religion* 8.4 (2009): 209–225.

21 See Alan J. Clark, " 'We believe in the gift of tongues': The 1906 Pentecostal Revolution and Its Effects on the LDS Use of the Gift of Tongues in the Twentieth Century," *Mormon Historical Studies* 14.1 (Spring 2013): 67–80; Matthew R. Davies, "The Tongues of the Saints: The Azusa Street Revival and the Changing Definition of Tongues," in *Joseph F. Smith: Reflections on the Man and His Times*, ed. Craig K. Manscill, Brian D. Reeves, Guy L. Dorius, and J. B. Haws. (Salt Lake City: Deseret Book, 2013), 470–485. For context, see Grant Wacker, *Heaven Below: Early Pentecostals and American Culture* (Cambridge, MA: Harvard University Press, 2001). Relief Society meetings in the 1920s were the last LDS Church settings for vernacular glossolalia. Although Heber J. Grant spoke publicly about glossolalia through the 1930s, he was careful to mention only nineteenth-century examples.

22 See Grant Underwood, *The Millenarian World of Early Mormonism* (Urbana: University of Illinois Press, 1999).

23 Nelson has made "hearkening"—listening with the intent to obey—a central message of his presidency; see "Hear Him," *Ensign* 50.5 (May 2020): 88–92.

10

SOMETHING WHISPERED

My narrative of the past—my mediation—has come full circle to an opening point: the most distinctive LDS sound is not any kind of music but a style of vocality that developed in conjunction with a major network music program. Across its entire history, Mormonism has consisted of old media revived through new media, from print editions of the "gold plates" to radio dictations of printed revelations to digital videos of radio broadcasts. More than 50 years after the passing of Richard Evans and nearly 100 years since his debut on the *Thoughtful Sabbath Hour*, members of the First Presidency and the Quorum of the Twelve stream in high-def video while speaking in a timbre and cadence derived from 1930s AM radio. The last apostle to speak in the pre-radio style—unscripted, overtime, with intensity and nasal twang—was the irrepressible LeGrand Richards, who died in 1983. His voice refused to be standardized. That is, he had the privilege, unlike, say, a term-limited Relief Society president, to disregard vocal correlation.

The correlated priesthood voice is noteworthy for its tempo: sedate, with long pauses. There is a feedback loop with priesthood succession, lifetime appointments, and vocal senescence. The original Council (now Quorum) of the Twelve Apostles in 1835 had an average age of thirty. That average reached fifty by 1863 and sixty by 1927, and it has remained above seventy since 1991.[1] The average age of the First Presidency is even higher. Because elderly people speak slower than young people, the LDS gerontocracy of the satellite broadcast era has taken the already measured style of middle-aged Evans and slowed it down even further. This sound of dignified infirmity has, in turn, been imitated by rising members of the Quorum of the Seventy who audition to become future prophets, seers, and revelators; stake presidents emulate those Seventies; and ambitious bishops imitate stake presidents. Streamed at 1.75× playback

https://doi.org/10.5876/781646427031.c010

speed, today's octogenarian and nonagenarian apostles can be made to sound "normal," but their pauses are still long. These silences—moments of wordlessness—may be their most distinctive sound. These are not dramatic, stylistic, or scripted pauses. Like those of Evans, they are programmatic.

By taking more time than necessary to communicate messages that are plain in meaning—a style of speech that non-believers may hear as mansplaining—senior General Authorities manifest their vocalic authority. Drawn-out slowness may also be a cover, for the Brethren are not (with rare exceptions) intellectuals, much less theologians. They are organization men. By pausing between their mundane words, they signal the mantle of their priesthood and the magnitude of their calling, trusting that listeners will fill in the gaps with faith. Over the course of hundreds of General Conference sessions, the Brethren have turned the Tabernacle and the Conference Center into gendered soundscapes. Women attending faithfully in silence have participated in this process. The LDS form of "sonic patriarchy" has nothing in common with catcalling and wolf-whistling, or blasting music from boom cars, or driving trucks with modified mufflers—nothing, that is, except the common male domination of aural space.[2]

Given that priesthood leaders act and dress in such plainly patriarchal ways, it is remarkable that they don't sound particularly masculine. With senescence, men speak at a higher pitch, just as women speak at a lower pitch. This biological fact combined with various cultural expressions—the guileless face, the missionary smile, the testimony tears—produces a gender paradox in contemporary Mormonism. The Brethren govern through meekness and quietude. Even as LDS women have lost power and "voice," the presiding elders' vocal effects and facial affects have become less manly. Rarely have homophobic men communicated such effeminacy.[3]

Reinforcing the soft slowness of priesthood speech, English is "naturally" slow-sounding compared to many languages—notably Spanish—because of its informational density, requiring fewer words and syllables per unit of speech.[4] Also, Anglophones from the Intermountain West speak less rapidly, with more pauses, than those from the East Coast, many of whom have immigrant ancestors from faster speech cultures with more syllable-intensive languages. Inevitably, LDS vocalization will diversify as more and more General Authorities rise in the ranks from non-US, non-white, non-Anglophone settings. It is happening already. The vicarious voice of Richard Evans is becoming fainter.

Then again, because the LDS Church is so assiduous about preserving its media records and reformatting and rebroadcasting them, the KSL cadence may linger for some time yet. In the radio era, Latter-day Saints were on the forefront of standardized American speech. Electrical transcription discs converted to magnetic tapes are now being converted to digital files—dead media revived, twice—by staff members and senior missionaries at the Church History Library. Believers can now stream the voices of all the prophets since Heber J. Grant. Even as the US media establishment has become lenient about accents, dialects, and code switching—and more welcoming of women and non-white people at the mike in the broadcast booth—the white LDS "priesthood voice" has been preserved for posterity. In this way, as in so many others, Mormons became "weird" again—even "queer" again—by holding on to mid-century normativity.[5]

A corollary follows. The second-most distinctive sound—or sound effect—in contemporary Mormonism is the continued silencing of women's vocality in public transmissions. Since Priesthood Correlation a half century ago, when anti-feminism became sanctified, the speaking time allotted to women in the main sessions of General Conference has consistently remained at 5 percent. And the Brethren command vocality on another level. In the LDS style of oratory, quotation is the order of the day, as evidenced by the many editions of *The Richard Evans Quotebook*. Conference speakers overwhelmingly quote priesthood men; in fact, women speakers rebroadcast men's voices even more than the Brethren do. From 1971 through 2020, a mere 2 percent of all quotations in Conference derived from women, and the majority of that modicum came from a single woman: Eliza R. Snow, "poetess" of the Restoration, blesser and healer of women, speaker and singer in tongues.[6]

Snow's anomalous vocal presence is hyper-pronounced, for her hymn lyric "O My Father" is one of the most performed songs of all time by the Salt Lake Tabernacle Choir. (A hymn setting was also a regular feature of John McClellan's early organ recitals.) Remarkably, Snow's rhyming lines are the quasi-doctrinal basis for Mother in Heaven—the eternal Father's partner, a co-deity implied by theological innovations Joseph Smith was working out at the time of his death. The choir sang Snow's poem in Chicago in 1893 and in San Francisco in 1896. When the choir returned to California in 1935, J. Reuben Clark insisted that the singing ambassadors go through all the verses. In the golden age of radio, the choir performed "O My Father" again and again on CBS despite the non-sectarian rule for sustaining programs. During the choir's explicit missionary tours in 1955 and 1958, "O My Father" was on the playbill at every concert. This was not by popular demand: the hymn failed to appear on Spencer Cornwall's 1958 list of selections of "widest acceptance," based on analysis of fan mail over thirty years.[7]

A brief history of "O My Father" thus provides a fitting coda to my inquiry into LDS music, vocality, and media.

The Church History Library has compiled a spreadsheet of the music performed in the Tabernacle and the Conference Center during General Conference weeks (first week in April, first week in October) from 1880 through 2020.[8] Over that 140-year period, "O My Father" was performed sixty-eight times, making it the fifteenth most popular hymn for the occasion. The number one hymn by a wide margin (262 performances) was "We Thank Thee, O God, for a Prophet," typically sung as a congregational number with augmentation by the choir. By contrast, "O My Father" was typically sung as a special number by visiting choirs and soloists, sometimes using an arrangement by Tracy Cannon. The song was sung solo because the lyrical point of view is far more personal than most in LDS hymnody.

The most unusual solo occurred in October 1900, when apostle Heber J. Grant reported on one of his self-improvement programs. He was, by his own account, tone deaf, but he loved hymns; he trained his vocal muscles mechanically, repeating the same song over and over up to 115 times a day, often playing along with one finger on the piano. "Six months ago I tried to sing 'O, My Father,' and failed," he reported from the pulpit. "I am going to try again, and if I fail tonight, I will try again each six months from now." He then succeeded in singing the song to the accompaniment of the Tabernacle Organ, played by Evan Stephens.[9]

Grant sang Snow's poem to the martial tune "Harwell," whereas Brigham Young had preferred the parlor song "Gentle Annie" by Stephen

Foster. Many settings were available, including the Haydn tune best known as "Deutschland, Deutschland über Alles," and one by LDS composer Thomas Durham, "Nephite Lamentation," written under the influence of the Holy Spirit. Stephens wrote two settings of "O My Father," but to his chagrin, a non-LDS tune—"I Will Sing of My Redeemer"—which he programmed for the 1893 dedication of the Salt Lake Temple, immediately became the popular favorite. He considered "My Redeemer" insipid, but he relented to demand and recorded an extra-slow, extra-sentimental version of it for the choir's first phonographic session in 1910. Much later, when the choir recorded its debut double LP on Columbia in 1949, it chose "O My Father" as one of the tracks, with future director Richard Condie as the solo tenor. Condie had started his career singing on KSL; he compared his "light" voice favorably to that of Bing Crosby.[10]

The setting "I Will Sing of My Redeemer," by James McGranahan, is a gospel hymn from the 1870s, when "gospel" was sung by white and Black Protestants alike. The original song, with lyrics by P. P. Bliss, is a nineteenth-century equivalent to "He," the swaying song of praise that Al Hibbler and the McGuire Sisters separately took to #7 and #12, respectively, on the Billboard Hot 100 in 1955. Whereas Snow's sentimental poem stresses the role of rationality in achieving personal revelation—"Truth is reason; truth eternal tells me I've a mother there"—Bliss's sentimental lyric is pure emotionality, a hymn of praise to Jesus and His "wondrous love to me." This is the kind of affecting song that many mid-century Mormons longed to sing, asked permission to sing—and were prohibited from singing. With the correlation of songbooks during the late 1940s, the Church Music Committee under Tracy Cannon removed most of the swaying tunes from the official hymnal, thus muting the musical traces of evangelicalism. But the revivalistic setting of "O My Father" was too familiar and beloved to excise.[11]

This hymn fills an absence in Mormonism, but it also reinforces silences. It matters that the only traditional and sanctioned way for Latter-day Saints to speak about Mother in Heaven is to sing about Her indirectly in a lyric centered on the Father. "When we sing that doctrinal hymn and anthem of affection," said President Spencer W. Kimball, "we get a sense of the ultimate in maternal modesty"—by which the prophet presumably meant quietude, even non-vocality.[12] Had Joseph Smith lived longer, he might have revealed something about Her voice; in this counterfactual, Mormons might have developed something comparable to Holy Mother worship in Catholicism and, with it, inspiration for a new genre of polytheistic hymns. "It's interesting that some women's names are acceptable to the Church and others aren't," wrote Leroy Robertson when working on the 1948 hymnal revision committee. "We Mormons can sing about 'Grace' all we want, but not about 'Mary.'"[13]

It's likely that most non-Mormon listeners to *Music and the Spoken Word* never registered the heterodoxy of Eliza R. Snow's lyric, which implies revelation to a woman as well as the existence of a female deity. In the poem, the voice of Snow speaks of another voice, "a secret something," that whispers to her the truth about the godhead. Snow biographer Jill Mulvay Derr said in an interview: "This concept of Heavenly Mother was certainly in the air when Eliza penned her hymn in fall 1845. I feel that she was a prophetess in the sense that she internalized this teaching, and the Spirit must have spoken to her in a particular way that confirmed its truth and gave her voice."[14] Derr, a historian employed by the Church, stood on a firm foundation, for Wilford Woodruff had said this in public: "That hymn is a revelation, though it was given unto us by a woman—Sister Snow. There are a great many sisters who have the spirit of revelation. There is no reason why they should not be inspired as well as men."[15] Heber J. Grant later said, in General Conference, that whenever he sang a hymn by Snow, he thanked God "for the gift of tongues to that noble woman," who had given him a blessing as a child foretelling he would become a leader in Zion, a divine message in glossolalia translated by Zina Young.[16]

According to post-correlation LDS belief and practice, with glossolalia all but suppressed, members of the Church may receive three types of personal revelation, in this order of frequency:

1. Indirectly through dreams.
2. Half-directly through the gift of the Holy Ghost, a "pure intelligence" that manifests as "sudden strokes of ideas" or promptings, or as gentle feelings like a nudge.
3. Directly through the Lord, who can introduce audible words into the mind as an acousmatic sound.

Strangely, the vocal identity of the "the Lord" in the Doctrine and Covenants is often ambiguous, without the Father or the Son specified. In the 1970s, Bruce R. McConkie attempted to clean up this theological untidiness and insisted (echoing James E. Talmage) that Latter-day Saints could not—in contradistinction to evangelicals—cultivate personal relationships with Jesus. However, even after Priesthood Correlation, LDS theology remains nebulous, and plenty of Saints hear voices other than that of the Father.[17]

For example: the former chief announcer of KSL, Paul Royall, a principled man who quit his job rather than read aloud advertisements for coffee, beer, and cigarettes—contravening two personal appeals from President David O. McKay to stay on the air—returned to voice work in retirement and, as an act of service to the Church, recorded the complete "standard works" (the four canonized scriptures) for release on audiotape in the late 1980s. Later, when speaking into a cassette recorder for an oral history interview to be transcribed and archived in the Church History Library, Brother Royall bore his testimony. "I know that Joseph Smith was a prophet," he said. "I have never seen him, but I've heard his voice, and I can tell you what it sounds like."[18]

No doubt, many Latter-day Saints have, over the decades, prayed to Heavenly Mother and heard a reply in their minds, though that kind of audition is not, as a rule, recorded and archived for posterity.[19] Goddess-to-human revelations cannot be intercepted or surveilled or blocked by priesthood gatekeepers, but neither can they be rebroadcast with amplification to a larger audience without the risk of disfellowshipment or excommunication.[20] God's wife remains the stillest, smallest voice in the Mormon soundsphere—a muted transmission from the great star Kolob—inaudible, perhaps, to all but well-tuned receivers.[21]

NOTES

1   Quentin Spencer, "Demographics of Apostles," April 25, 2023, LDS Data Analysis blog, https://qhspencer.github.io/lds-data-analysis/apostles.

2   I borrow this phrase from Rebecca Lentjes, Amy E. Alterman, and Whitney Arey, "'The Ripping Apart of Silence': Sonic Patriarchy and Anti-Abortion Harassment," *Resonance* 1.4 (Winter 2020): 422–442.

3   See Kathryn Lofton, "A Brief History of the Mormon Smile," *Journal of Mormon History* 50.1 (Winter 2024): 21–46; Johnson, *Mormons, Musical Theater, and Belonging in America.*

4   See Christophe Coupé, Yoon Mi Oh, Dan Dediu, and François Pellegrino, "Different Languages, Similar Encoding Efficiency: Comparable Information Rates across the Human Communicative Niche," *Science Advances* 5 (September 4, 2019): eaaw2594; Pedro Aceves and James A. Evans, "Human Languages with Greater Information Density Have Higher Communication Speed but Lower Conversation Breadth," *Nature Human Behaviour* 8 (April 2024): 644–656.

5   See K. Mohrman, *Exceptionally Queer: Mormon Peculiarity and U.S. Nationalism* (Minneapolis: University of Minnesota Press, 2022).

6   Eliza Wells, "Quoted at the Pulpit: Male Rhetoric and Female Authority in Fifty Years of General Conference," *Dialogue* 55.4 (Winter 2022): 1–40. For context, see Colleen McDannell, *Sister Saints: Mormon Women since the End of Polygamy* (New York: Oxford University Press, 2018).

7   *Century of Singing*, 401–410. Snow originally titled her poem "My Father in Heaven" (1845), later revised to "Invocation, or the Eternal Father and Mother" (1856).

8   General Conference music data set.

9   *Seventy-first Semi-annual Conference* (Salt Lake City: Deseret News, 1900), 74.

10 Richard P. Condie, interviewed by Jerold D. Ottley, March 1978–September 1982, OH 656, 17, Church History Library (CHL).

11 See Michael Hicks, "'O My Father': The Musical Settings," *BYU Studies* 36.1 (1996–1997): 32–57. Another anomalous selection, "How Great Thou Art," made it into to the 1985 hymnal due to personal lobbying by apostles Thomas S. Monson and Ezra Taft Benson, who loved this particular "praise" or "worship" song even though the Brethren had steered the Church away from that genre.

12 Spencer W. Kimball, "The True Way of Life and Salvation" (General Conference talk), *Ensign* 8 (May 1978): 4–7, quote on 6.

13 Wilson, *Leroy Robertson*, 272.

14 Cherry Bushman Silver, "Making the Acquaintance of Eliza R. Snow: An Interview with Her Biographer, Jill Mulvay Derr," *BYU Studies* 59.3 (2020): 151–176, quote on 161. For context, see Linda P. Wilcox, "The Mormon Concept of a Mother in Heaven," in Beecher and Anderson, *Sisters in Spirit*, 64–77.

15 "Discourse by President Wilford Woodruff, October 8, 1893 (in Salt Lake)," *Millennial Star* 56.15 (April 9, 1894): 229.

16 *Eighty-fourth Annual Semi-annual Conference* (Salt Lake City: Deseret News, 1913), 92. Grant recounted this incident many times, including again at General Conference in 1927.

17 See "To Hear the Voice of the Lord," in *Teachings of Presidents of the Church: Harold B. Lee* (Salt Lake City: The Church of Jesus Christ of Latter-day Saints, 2011), 48–58; Tom Mould, *Still, the Small Voice: Narrative, Personal Revelation, and the Mormon Folk Tradition* (Logan: Utah State University Press, 2011). For specific context, see Stirling Adams, "The End of Bruce R. McConkie's *Mormon Doctrine*," *John Whitmer Historical Association Journal* 32.2 (Fall–Winter 2012): 59–69. For general context, T. M. Luhrmann, *When God Talks Back: Understanding the American Evangelical Relationship with God* (New York: Knopf, 2012).

18   Paul F. Royall, interviewed by Brian Sokolowsky, November 17, 1998, OH 1910, 15, CHL.

19   A noteworthy exception is Teddie Wood Porter, "Uttered or Unexpressed" (letter to the editor), *Dialogue* 9.3 (Autumn 1974): 7, which recounts "a wondrous voice clearly answered"; see also the reply, Karen Sorenson Smith, "Truth Is Reason, Truth Eternal" (letter to the editor), *Dialogue* 9.4 (Winter 1974): 5.

20   These disciplinary terms have recently been retired in favor of "formal membership restriction" and "withdrawal of membership."

21   For descriptions of Kolob, see Abraham 3:1–28 from the Pearl of Great Price. On March 17, 2024, the Church Communication Department posted a short video on Instagram, featuring Relief Society first counselor Anette Dennis, who said: "There is no other religious organization in the world, that I know of, that has so broadly given power and authority to women." In response to this priesthood-approved proxy message from a member of a presidency with no power, thousands of LDS women posted comments—an unprecedented outpouring that caught the attention of the *New York Times*. These social media comments carried no sound, but one could still hear sorrow, disillusionment, anger, hurt, humiliation, and occasional strains of hope.